Holding in Trust

Hope Publishing Company
CAROL STREAM IL 60188

Published by Hope Publishing Co., Carol Stream, Ill. 60188.

Publishers Reprint Notice

The Hymn Society is eager to have these hymns introduced and sung widely. For permission to reprint any of these texts or tunes, please contact Hope Publishing Co., which serves as copyright agent for The Hymn Society. Permission can be granted for individual hymns (usually for a nominal fee), or an annual licensing agreement can provide blanket permission for any or all of these hymns. Contact Hope Publishing Co.'s Copyright Desk at 380 S. Main Pl., Carol Stream, IL 60188, (708) 665-3200.

Code No. 1097

Typeset and designed by Selah Publishing Co., Inc.

First edition
2 3 4 5 6 7 8 9 10 95 94 93 92

ISBN 0-916642-46-1
Library of Congress Catalog Card Number: 92-071634

Contents

Introduction

The Hymn Society in the United States and Canada has been publishing new hymns since it began in 1922, seventy years ago this year. Of the thousands of hymns submitted on various subjects, hundreds were chosen by judges and editors for hymn searches and competitions. The best were published in pamphlets or in *The Hymn*, the quarterly journal of the society. Many of those hymns have since been included in hymnals across North America and beyond, some in translation. But many others have been forgotten. We found many worthy hymns buried in back issues of *The Hymn* and in little booklets long out of print.

In a continuing effort to serve hymnal committees, churches, and all those who love hymns, we offer this collection of some of the best hymns The Hymn Society has published through 1991. These 115 texts and 28 tunes in no way comprise a complete hymnal; indeed, in some ways they complement the typical hymnal. Where many hymnals have few hymns, for example, dealing with ecology, ecumenism, or global and urban concerns of peace and justice, this collection has several. The Hymn Society has always sponsored hymn searches to fill gaps and address concerns not met in available hymns.

Our thanks to the many authors and composers who contributed to this collection. We provided what information about them we could find; in some cases all we had was a name, with no dates. Because language sensitivities regarding inclusivity and even specific word meanings have changed so profoundly in the last generation, we altered (marked "alt.") several texts, sometimes changing pronouns, and at times omitting stanzas. In every case, the source of the original is indicated.

The complete set of indexes will make this collection useful to hymnal committees and those pastors and musicians who select hymns for worship services. In addition, we have prepared for the first time a combined index of all thirty-three collections published by The Hymn Society. This collection index along with *The Hymn* indexes will provide access to all the hymns held in trust by The Hymn Society.

We now entrust these hymns to a wider public, with the hope that they may move from these pages into church bulletins, into new hymnals, and—most of all—to the voices and hearts of those who continue to sing new songs to our Creator.

The Hymn Society in the United States and Canada
Editorial Committee

George Black
Emily R. Brink
Nancy R. Faus
April 1992

Hymn Texts and Music

Codes

H82	*The Hymnal 1982*
HB	*The Hymn Book of the Anglican Church of Canada and the United Church of Canada*
HWB	*Hymnal: A Worship Book*
PH	*The Presbyterian Hymnal*
PsH	*Psalter Hymnal*
RL	*Rejoice in the Lord*
UM	*The United Methodist Hymnal*
WC	*The Worshiping Church*

A Bird, a Lovely Butterfly

88 86

A bird, a lovely butterfly,
a fleecy cloud up in the sky,
a mighty mountain, wide and high,
all speak of you, O God.

A daisy, rose or daffodil,
the green grass growing on the hill,
the woodlands friendly, deep and still,
all speak of you, O God.

For gentle rain, the quiet snow,
for sun and moon and starlight glow,
for all the beauty that we know,
our thanks to you, O God.

Words: Florence Jansson, alt. (b. 1896)
Source: "Twelve New Hymns for Children," 1965;
The Hymn 20:124 (October 1969)
Possible tunes: WOODLANDS (see p. 174),
SIXTH NIGHT (H82 250)
Scriptural reference: Psalm 19:1-6
Topics: Children, Creation, Gratitude

As Children of One God

CM

As children of one God we must
  believe we all have worth;
regardless of the tongue we speak
  or of our place of birth.

In Christ his Son, we know we're one,
  and that he died for all;
each culture has some good to share
  in answering his call.

He only asks that love inspire
  and motivate our deeds,
so we can help fulfill his wish
  for all, in all their needs.

We all possess God-given powers
  to think and plan and feel;
now let us seek the ones who hurt
  so we may help and heal.

As children of one God we must
  be joined in his employ
to help extend Christ's ministry
  of healing love and joy.

Words: Muriel Keenze (1891-1981)
Source: "Nine Hymns for Human Relations Day," 1977
Possible tune: DUNDEE
Scriptural references: Galatians 3:28, I Thessalonians 1:3
Topics: Ecumenism, Healing, Human Relations, Unity, Witnessing

As He Gathered at His Table

87 87

As he gathered at his table
those who longed to know the way,
Christ proclaimed a holy mystery;
still his words call us today.

As he took the towel and basin,
not as master, but as friend,
Christ portrayed the way of service;
still in serving we must bend.

As he blessed the bread and broke it,
human need to satisfy,
Christ made even traitors welcome;
still we question "Is it I?"

As he took the cup and shared it,
telling of the Father's care,
Christ poured out himself in promise;
still that covenant we must share.

As they sang a hymn together,
praising Israel's saving King,
hearts and voices made one music;
still delivering love we sing.

As he went into the garden
praying, "Father, use your Son,"
Christ alone could know its meaning;
still we pray, "God's will be done."

Though this feast be one of symbols,
what we celebrate is real;
still Christ welcomes to his table;
still Christ serves us at his meal.

Words: Paul A. Richardson, 1986 (b. 1951)
Source: *The Worshiping Church,* no. 778
Possible tune: STUART (see p. 166)
Scriptural references: Matthew 26:17-30, Matthew 26:36-46, Mark 14:17-26, Mark 14:32-42, Luke 22:14-23, Luke 22:39-46, John 13:1-17
Topic: Communion

As Saints of Old Their First Fruits Brought*

CMD

As saints of old their first fruits brought
 of orchard, flock, and field
to God the giver of all good,
 the source of bounteous yield;
so we today first fruits would bring:
 the wealth of this good land,
of farm and market, shop and home,
 of mind, and heart, and hand.

A world in need now summons us
 to labor, love, and give;
to make our life an offering
 that others too may live.
The Church of Christ is calling us
 to make the dream come true:
a world redeemed, your kingdom come,
 all life in Christ made new.

In gratitude and humble trust
 we bring our best today,
to serve your cause and share your love
 with all humanity.
O God, who gave yourself to us
 in Jesus Christ your Son,
teach us to give ourselves each day
 until life's work is done.

*Original first line: As men of old their first fruits brought

Words: Frank von Christierson, alt. (b. 1900)
Source: "Ten New Stewardship Hymns," 1961
Possible tune: REGWAL (PsH 294)
Scriptural references: Proverbs 3:9, Romans 12:1-2, James 1:17
Topics: Gratitude, Mission, Offering, Stewardship, Unity

As They Before Thine Altar Bow

LM

As they before thine altar bow
we pray that thou wilt bless them now,
and may their marriage ever be
a union hallowed, Lord, by thee.

As here each solemn vow they take,
we seek thy strength, that they may make
their hearts and home thy dwelling-place,
their lives a witness to thy grace.

As years go by may they fulfill
the purpose of thy holy will,
and faithfully with one accord
serve Christ, our ever-living Lord.

Words: Franklin P. Frye (1903-1984)
Source: "Thirteen New Marriage and Family Life Hymns," 1961
Possible tune: MELCOMBE
Topics: Commitment, Home and Family,
Weddings/Christian Marriage

Break Forth, O Living Light of God

CM

Break forth, O living light of God,
upon the world's dark hour!
Show us the way the Master trod;
reveal his saving power.

Remove the veil of ancient words,
their message long obscure;
restore to us your truth, O God,
and make its meaning sure.

Show us the servants from your word,
the women and the men,
who kept the faith and walked with you;
O make them live again!

O let your word be light anew
to every nation's life;
unite us in your will, O Lord,
and end all sinful strife.

O may one Lord, one faith, one word,
one Spirit lead us still;
and one great Church go forth in might
to work God's perfect will.

Words: Frank von Christierson, alt. (b. 1900)
Source: "Ten New Hymns on the Bible," 1952
Possible tune: ST. PETER
Scriptural references: Ephesians 4:4-6, Hebrews 11
Topics: Saints, Word of God

Christ Found a World Divided

76 76 D

Christ found a world divided
 by culture, color, creed;
he loved them all, he joined them
 by word and helpful deed.
He drew them all together—
 that man of Galilee—
all peoples, tribes, and races,
 united and yet free.

And still the work continues:
 this is our dream, our goal:
to bring the world together
 in one united whole.
Each human life respected,
 each culture and each taste,
each background and each viewpoint;
 none scorned in pride or haste.

Respecting each one's talent,
 concern for each one's need—
to some much has been given:
 from some we much received—
some offer fun and music;
 some bring their strength and skill;
some boast artistic genius;
 some gifts of mind and will.

United by our caring
 for each and everyone;
united by our Savior,
 by Christ, the Holy One:
all human life is sacred;
 no human life is dross.
Lead on, O Christ, we follow
 as comrades of the cross.

Words: Frank von Christierson (b. 1900)
Source: "Nine Hymns for Human Relations Day," 1977
Possible tune: ELLACOMBE
Scriptural references: Luke 12:48, Galatians 3:28,
 Ephesians 2:14-18
Topics: Ecumenism, Gifts, Human Relations, Unity

Christ Is Risen! Raise Your Voices

87 87 D

Christ is risen! Raise your voices
jubilant with joy and praise.
Christ is risen! Earth rejoices!
To the Lord your anthems raise.
Over sin and death victorious,
Christ is risen! Hail your King!
Ever may his praise be glorious;
let the world his triumph sing!

Lord of life, our Savior risen,
bid the shadows flee away;
death no more a darkened prison,
death the door to life's new day.
This the resurrection chorus,
lift its music on the air:
Jesus lives, our Lord victorious.
Tell it! Tell it everywhere.

Life eternal! joy of heaven;
life abundant — joy of earth;
life which God in Christ has given
brings to us new hope, new worth.
Lift your hearts from sin and sadness,
trust this joyful sacred word,
fill the earth with holy gladness:
Christ is risen! Christ our Lord!

Words: Frank von Christierson (b. 1900)
Source: *The Hymn* 22:45 (April 1971)
Possible tunes: LOWELL (PsH 406), HYMN TO JOY
Topics: Easter/Resurrection, Jesus Christ

Christmas Bells with Joy Are Ringing

87 87 D

Christmas bells with joy are ringing,
  telling forth that Christ is born!
Hail, the Son of God incarnate,
  welcome to the heavenly dawn!
See! His light is shining brighter
  than the star which gleams above;
radiancy divine unending,
  springing from eternal love!

Love has come to guide our footsteps,
  Love has come to point the way,
Love supreme and everlasting,
  Love has come to help us pray.
Let us with triumphant voices
  joyfully our anthems sing:
Jesus Christ has come to save us!
  Praise to our Redeemer King!

Holy Babe, we humbly offer
  heart and soul and mind to thee,
show us by thy Holy Spirit
  all that thou wouldst have us be;
may our love reflect the wonder
  of thy selfless love divine,
and our lives in glad surrender
  evermore be wholly thine!

Words: Violet Buchanan, alt.
Source: "New Hymns, Songs, and Prayers for
  Church and Home," 1974
Possible tune: VESPER HYMN (PsH 484)
Topics: Christmas, Love

Come Now and Praise the Humble Saint

CM with alleluias

Come now and praise the humble saint
of David's house and line,
the carpenter whose life fulfilled
our gracious God's design.
Alleluia, Alleluia.

The Architect's high miracles
he saw, and what was done,
the virgin's spouse, the guardian of
great David's greater Son.
Alleluia, Alleluia.

To him the angel told in dreams
his God's most loving deed;
he lived in full obedience,
the part of him — to heed.
Alleluia! Rejoice! His part to heed.

With him the holy virgin lived,
a maid blest from above;
he knew in perfect charity
the share for him — to love.
Alleluia! Rejoice! His part to love.

By him the Son was meekly raised
to be on earth a friend;
he taught his pure humility,
the task for him — to tend.
Alleluia! Rejoice! His part to tend.

For him there was no glory here,
    no crown or martyr's fame,
for him there was the patient life
    of faith and humble name.
    Alleluia! Alleluia!

But now within the Father's grace
    where saints and angels throng
beside his spouse, before the Son,
    he sings the glorious song:
    Alleluia! Alleluia!

Words: George W. Williams (b. 1922)
Source: *The Hymn* 30:284 (October 1979)
Possible tune: SEWANEE (*The Hymn,* October, 1979)
Scriptural reference: Matthew 1:18-25
Topics: Advent, Jesus Christ, Saints

Cradled in a Manger

65 65

Cradled in a manger,
on the fragrant hay,
lo, the Christ lay sleeping
on that holy day.

Shepherds on the hillsides
saw a wondrous sight;
heard the angel's message,
"Christ is born this night."

Hastened they their footsteps,
found him in a stall,
worshiped there adoring
Christ, the Lord of all.

Wise men travelled to him,
guided by a star,
over plain and desert
from a country, far;

offered gifts and worship,
lowly kneeling there,
to the little Christ Child,
Son of God most fair.

Come we too this Christmas,
by his great love led;
bringing love and worship
to his manger bed.

Words: Frances Martha Hubbert alt.
Source: "Twelve New Hymns for Children," 1965;
The Hymn 17:112 (October 1966)
Possible tunes: CRADLED (*The Hymn*, October 1966),
EUDOXIA (HB 122), MERRIAL (H82 42)
Scriptural references: Matthew 2:1-12, Luke 2:1-20
Topics: Children, Christmas, Epiphany

Creating God, Your Fingers Trace

LM

Creating God, your fingers trace
the bold designs of farthest space;
let sun and moon and stars and light
and what lies hidden praise your might.

Sustaining God, your hands uphold
earth's mysteries known or yet untold;
let water's fragile blend with air,
enabling life, proclaim your care.

Redeeming God, your arms embrace
all now oppressed for creed or race;
let peace, descending like a dove,
make known on earth your healing love.

Indwelling God, your gospel claims
one family with a billion names;
let every life be touched by grace
until we praise you face to face.

Words: Jeffery Rowthorn, 1974 (b. 1934)
Source: *The Hymn* 30:128 (April 1979)
Possible tunes: KILLIBEGS (PsH 605), KEDRON (H82 163),
DEUS TUORUM MILITUM (HWB),
CHRISTOPHER DOCK (HWB)
Scriptural references: Genesis 1, Psalm 19:1-6
Topics: Adoration and Praise, Creation, Healing, Peace,
Stewardship, Social Concerns, Trinity, Unity

Creative Life, When You Spoke Forth

CMD

Creative Life, when you spoke forth
great power surged on high;
your signature of galaxies
was blazed across the sky.
You set the planets in their paths
and formed our lives with skill:
O recreate, till all rejoice
to orbit in your will!

Redeeming Life, your love was shown
while living here on earth:
unyielding, unrelenting love
which gives our souls new birth;
undying love, though crucified—
what luxury of grace!
So let our love abound till all
are sure of your embrace.

Enabling Life, whose Spirit seeks
the oft-fragmented soul,
unite all segments of our lives
till we are fully whole.
When Christians lived in true accord
your Holy Spirit came;
grant unity and power today,
and set our hearts aflame!

Eternal Life, to whom we rise,
your wisdom shows us how
the deeds of truly risen lives
serve people here and now.
Though burdens often weigh us down
our faith and hope still soar
till love draws us to life with you
both now and evermore!

Words: David A. Robb (b. 1932)
Source: *The Hymn* 34:155 (July 1983)
Possible tune: ELLACOMBE
Scriptural references: Genesis 1, Acts 2:1-4
Topics: Creation, Trinity, Unity

Creator God, We Give You Thanks

LM

Creator God, we give you thanks
for all the glories you have made.
Help us to see you in your work,
the Artist in the art displayed.

As we survey your handiwork,
restrain our minds from petty greed.
Respect before your great design
is reverence paid to you indeed.

What you have given us in trust
is only ours to rightly use.
Deliver us from thoughtless deeds
that plunder, pillage, and abuse.

Help us to see your draftsman's hand
in every blade of grass, each flower,
that we may stand in awe before
the work of your creative power.

Words: Betty Anne J. Arner
Source: "Sixteen New Hymns on The Stewardship of the Environment," 1973
Possible tune: WAREHAM (H82 20)
Scriptural references: Psalm 8, Psalm 19:1-6
Topics: Creation, Ecology/Environment, Gratitude, Stewardship, Thanksgiving

Dear Lord, You Are Power

11 11 11 11

Dear Lord, you are power and wisdom and might,
our source of salvation, our truest delight,
our hope for tomorrow, our joy for today,
the truth and the glory we share on our way.

If this is our life-theme, if this we confess,
then send us with comfort to bind up distress.
If you are our citadel, courage, and song,
then send us to battle all evil and wrong.

Come, Love, and compel us to honor our creeds.
Come, Mercy, and lead us to meet human needs.
The world has been fractured, its healing is late,
the times are in darkness, the sorrow is great.

Lord, make of us instruments tuned to your peace,
proclaiming redemption, uplifting release,
release from sin's burden, from poverty's grief,
with fresh air of freedom, with joy and relief.

Dear Lord, be our power and wisdom and might,
our source of salvation, our truest delight,
our hope for tomorrow, our joy for today,
the truth and the glory we share on our way.

Words: David G. Mehrtens (b. 1930)
Source: *The Hymn* 42:43 (January 1991)
Possible tune: RUSSELL (see p. 156)
Topics: Peace, Power of God, Truth, Wisdom

Elusive God

10 10 10 10

Elusive God, escaping every phrase
that tries to perfectly describe your ways,
we catch a glimpse of you and choose a word
so clear to one but to another, blurred.

If easy words serve only to confuse,
then we must find fresh images to use,
and may that earnest quest for concepts new
reveal not merely words, but more of you.

Words: Dorothy R. Fulton
Source: *The Hymn* 41:2 (April 1990)
Possible tunes: SONG 24, LANGRAN
Topics: Image of God, Justice

Eternal Christ, Who, Kneeling

76 76 D

Eternal Christ, who, kneeling
    when earthly tasks were done,
turned unto God appealing,
    "That they may all be one,"
we thank you for your vision
    of unity untorn,
of faith without division
    with which your church was born.

But we have often slighted
    the ties designed to hold
your followers united
    within one common fold.
Writ dark on history's pages
    we see, O Lord, with shame,
the strife which through the ages
    has marred your church's name.

Accept our deep contrition
    for all our sundering ways
which still disrupt your mission,
    which mock our words of praise.
Lord, may your Spirit guide us
    that we may find, beyond
the things which still divide us,
    love's all-embracing bond.

In this our generation
    make fruitful, Lord, our search
for reconciliation
    of all within your church.
Redeemed from her unfitness,
    Lord, may the church, your bridge,
as one proclaim her witness,
    as one with you abide.

Words: William W. Reid, Jr. (b. 1923)
Source: *The Hymn* 27:57 (April 1976)
Possible tune: NYLAND (PsH 285)
Scriptural reference: John 17:20-23
Topics: Church, Confession, Jesus Christ, Reconciliation, Unity

Eternal Spirit of the Living Christ

10 10 10 10

Eternal Spirit of the living Christ,
I know not how to ask or what to say;
I only know my need, as deep as life,
and only you can teach me how to pray.

Come, pray in me the prayer I need this day;
help me to see your purpose and your will —
where I have failed, what I have done amiss;
held in forgiving love, let me be still.

Come with the strength I lack, the vision clear
of neighbor's need, of all humanity;
fulfillment of my life in love outpoured;
my life in you, O Christ; your love in me.

Words: Frank von Christierson (b. 1900)
Source: "New Hymns, Songs, and Prayers for Church and Home," 1974; *The Hymn* 25:1 (January 1975)
Possible tunes: NYACK (H82 318), CLIFFTOWN (HB 251)
Scriptural reference: Romans 8:26-27
Topics: Guidance, Holy Spirit, Prayer

Father Eternal, We Pray for Your Blessing

11 10 11 10

Father Eternal, we pray for your blessing,
kneeling before you, Creator of love,
need for your strength, for your guidance, confessing,
grant that our union be blessed from above.

Bind us together in constant affection,
lead us and guard us and keep us from strife;
stretch forth your hand to provide our direction;
show us together the pathway of life.

O God, we pray that through life you will guide us,
while all our joys and our sorrows we share;
wisdom, devotion, and patience provide us.
Keep our love strong in your sheltering care.

Words: Josephine D. Reinhardt, alt. (b. 1921)
Source: "Thirteen New Marriage and Family Life Hymns," 1961
Possible tune: O QUANTA QUALIA (PsH 235)
Topics: Guidance, Prayer, Weddings/Christian Marriage

For All the Love

10 10 10 with alleluias

For all the love that in our life abounds,
for all the beauty that this world surrounds,
for music which so joyfully resounds,
    Alleluia, Alleluia!

For all the love of family and friends,
and for the love which God in mercy sends,
for all the love toward others God intends,
    Alleluia, Alleluia!

For all God's love to bless this pair today,
for all God's love to guide them on their way,
for all God's love and joy and peace we pray,
    Alleluia, Alleluia!

Words: Creighton Lacy
Source: *The Hymn* 26:70 (July 1975)
Possible tunes: FREDERICKTOWN, ENGELBERG,
    SINE NOMINE
Topics: Love, Weddings/Christian Marriage

For Each Day of Life We Thank You

87 87

For each day of life we thank you,
   Lord, the giver of all days;
and with hearts filled with thanksgiving,
   we would serve you, Lord, always.

As in days of youthful vigor,
   may we in all later years
know the joys of useful purpose.
   Free us, Lord, from anxious fears.

Give us dreams and inner vision
   of a new world to be gained,
where all people live together,
   by each other's love sustained.

May the insights gained from living
   be a light upon the way,
guiding us, and those to follow,
   to a brighter, better day.

Words: H. Glen Lanier, alt. (1925-1978)
Source: "Ten New Hymns on Aging and the Later Years," 1976
Possible tunes: KINGDOM (PsH 302), GALILEE (PH 398)
Topics: Aging, Gratitude, Guidance, Thanksgiving

For Your True Church

10 10 10 10

For your true Church we lift our hearts in prayer,
come to us now and your own strength impart,
that we may sense your presence with us here,
and worship you with all our mind and heart.

Pour forth your Spirit on your servants now;
help them proclaim the gospel of your grace;
kindle their souls whene'er in prayer they bow,
and may they all your holy faith embrace.

Anoint their lips that they may speak your word;
true to their call, may they their task fulfill;
from all distrust and error, free them, Lord;
make them true prophets of your holy will.

Words: Henry Burnham Kirkland, alt. (b. 1884)
Source: "Ten New Hymns on the Ministry," 1966
Possible tunes: LANGRAN (PsH 74), TOULON (H82 359)
Topics: Church, Holy Spirit/Pentecost, Ministry, Prayer, Witnessing, Worship

Forgive, O Lord, Our Sins So Great

LM

Forgive, O Lord, our sins so great:
of your good gifts, our grave misuse,
by which your earth we desecrate
and deadly perils help produce.

For foul pollution of our air,
of water, land—so long ignored—
for simply being unaware
of damage done, forgive us, Lord.

Have mercy on us, Lord, we pray,
for blight of nature's wondrous art:
that we your providence betray
we would confess with shameful heart.

Help us use well for human need
your rich resources, lest they be
exhausted by our sin and greed.
While time remains, Lord, hear our plea.

Words: Donald H. Brown, alt.
Source: "Sixteen New Hymns on the Stewardship of the Environment," 1973
Possible tune: MELCOMBE
Topics: Confession, Ecology/Environment, Forgiveness

From Hearts Around the World

LM

From hearts around the world, O Lord,
through centuries of blind discord,
there is one prayer which does not cease;
the people yearn and grope for peace.

Though war and hate have been our lot,
the dream, the hope, of peace die not.
Let nothing move our hearts from thee,
apart from whom no peace can be.

Lord, use thy Church to point the way;
may we thy clear commands obey:
be reconciled, forgive, and bless;
may peace proceed from righteousness.

Lord, we confess our greed and pride,
the scorn of those for whom Christ died,
the prejudice, neglect, and hate,
the love of wealth and power too great.

Grant us our Master's heart and mind,
his care for all the poor and blind,
for every race, for young and old,
despised, rejected, hungry, cold.

Let us not lose the vision blest,
the dream of peace, the hope, the quest;
thy gracious will be done each day;
thy kingdom come on earth, we pray.

Words: Elizabeth Patton Moss
Source: "Twelve New World Order Hymns," 1958
Possible tune: KEDRON (H82 163)
Scriptural references: Matthew 6:10, Luke 11:2
Topics: Confession, Peace, Social Concerns/Welfare,
Witnessing, World Order

Glorious Is Thy Name, Most Holy

87 87 D

Glorious is thy Name, Most Holy,
God and Father of us all;
we thy servants bow before thee,
strive to answer every call.
Thou with life's great good hast blest us,
cared for us from earliest years;
unto thee our thanks we render;
thy deep love o'ercomes all fears.

For our world of need and anguish
we would lift to thee our prayer.
Faithful stewards of thy bounty,
may we with our neighbors share.
In the name of Christ our Savior
who redeems and sets us free,
gifts we bring of heart and treasure,
that our lives may worthier be.

In the midst of time we journey,
from thy hand comes each new day;
we would use it in thy service,
humbly, wisely, while we may.
So to thee, Lord and Creator,
praise and honor we accord—
thine the earth and thine the heavens,
through all time the Eternal Word.

Words: Ruth Elliott, alt.
Source: "Ten New Stewardship Hymns," 1961
Possible tunes: IN BABILONE, AUSTRIAN HYMN
Topics: Prayer, Righteousness, Servanthood, Stewardship, Thanksgiving

Go Forth, Strong Word of God

SM

Go forth, strong word of God;
the lamp of life thou art.
Bring love of truth and righteousness
to every human heart.

Go forth, strong word of God;
thou shalt not know defeat.
Revive the Church's martyr zeal,
her glorious task complete.

Go forth, strong word of God;
forever shalt thou stand.
Redeem our nation; let it be
a strong and holy land.

Go forth, strong word of God;
make this a glorious hour.
Send out the light till all shall know
the Spirit's wondrous power.

Words: Frank LeRoy Cross, 1952, alt. (b. 1904)
Source: "Ten New Hymns on the Bible," 1952
Possible tune: ST. THOMAS
Scriptural reference: Psalm 119:105
Topics: Righteousness of God, Truth, Word of God

God Almighty, God Eternal

87 87 D

God almighty, God eternal,
to your throne we bring our prayer,
asking help and seeking guidance
for your people everywhere.
In this age of changing boundaries,
widening space, and spreading sphere,
give to us the strength to follow
when your will for us is clear.

God unchanging, God forever,
in these times of sky and space,
when has come a new dimension
to our wide-spread human race,
lend to us your understanding,
loving spirit, fervent zeal,
that our daily, living witness
may be filled with Christ's appeal.

God the Sovereign, our Creator,
God to whom all things belong,
ever speaking through the ages
to the universal throng,
speak again to all your children,
voice your truth to us, we pray,
as the world of nature widens,
teach us how to live Christ's way.

Words: Mary Jackson Cathey, alt. (b. 1926)
Source: "Twelve New World Order Hymns," 1958
Possible tunes: ABBOT'S LEIGH, AUSTRIA, GENEVA (PH 73)
Topics: Guidance, Image of God, Prayer, Sovereignty of God, World Order

God Gave to Me a Life to Live

LM

God gave to me a life to live;
God gave me hands, with which to give;
God gave a heart with which to care;
God gave me love that I might share.

When I am helped to see what's good,
and led to do the things I should,
I thank you, Father, God above,
for life and hands and heart and love.

Words: Jean Edwards Learn
Source: "Twelve New Hymns for Children," 1965
Possible tune: WINCHESTER NEW
Topics: Children, Service/Servanthood, Thanksgiving

God Has Spoken by the Prophets

87 87 D

God has spoken by the prophets,
  spoken the unchanging Word;
each from age to age proclaiming
  God the One, the righteous Lord!
'Mid the world's despair and turmoil
  one firm anchor holding fast:
God eternal reigns forever,
  God the first and God the last.

God has spoken by Christ Jesus,
  Christ, the everlasting Son,
brightness of the Father's glory,
  with the Father ever one;
spoken by the Word incarnate,
  God of God ere time was born;
Light of Light, to earth descending,
  Christ, as God in human form.

God is speaking by the Spirit,
  speaking to our hearts again,
in the age-long word declaring
  God's own message, now as then.
Through the rise and fall of nations
  one sure faith is standing fast:
God abides, the Word unchanging,
  God the first and God the last.

Words: George Wallace Briggs, alt. (1875-1959)
Source: "Ten New Hymns on the Bible," 1952
Possible tune: EBENEZER
Scriptural references: John 1:1-5, John 1:14, Hebrews 1:1-3,
  Hebrews 6:19, Revelation 1:17, Revelation 22:13
Topics: Kingdom of God, Trinity, Word of God

God in His Love for Us

11 10 11 10 Dactylic

God in his love for us lent us this planet,
gave it a purpose in time and in space:
small as a spark from the fire of creation,
cradle of life and the home of our race.

Thanks be to God for its bounty and beauty,
life that sustains us in body and mind:
plenty for all, if we learn how to share it,
riches undreamed of to fathom and find.

Long have our human wars ruined its harvest;
long has earth bowed to the terror of force.
Long have we wasted what others have need of,
poisoned the fountain of life at its source.

Earth is the Lord's: it is ours to enjoy it,
ours, as his stewards, to farm and defend.
Now from pollution, misuse, and destruction,
good Lord, deliver us, world without end!

Words: Fred Pratt Green (b. 1903)
Source: "Sixteen New Hymns on the Stewardship of the Environment," 1973
Possible tunes: RUSSIAN HYMN, LIEBSTER EMMANUEL, O QUANTA QUALIA
Scriptural reference: Psalm 24:1
Topics: Creation, Earth, Ecology/Environment, Stewardship

God of All, Whose Love Surrounds Us

87 87 87

God of all, whose love surrounds us,
we unite in praise of thee,
one in heart and one in purpose,
one in Christian love to be.
Lord, awake us to the vision
of a world redeemed and free!

Thou hast led us by thy Spirit
to accept thy kingdom's goal.
Hand in hand with joy advancing,
we are one in heart and soul,
filled by thee with one great passion:
that the world may be made whole.

Grant us, in the mind's maturing,
thine own guidance on our way.
Purge our hearts from hate and envy;
quench the pride that may hold sway;
quicken us with power abundant
for the work we face today.

Let us then our service render,
witnessing thy love for all,
toiling with unceasing fervor,
swift to venture at thy call.
Make us in thy strength victorious
with our Christ, the Lord of all.

Words: Daniel B. Merrick, Jr. (b. 1926)
Source: "Five New Hymns for Youth By Youth," 1955
Possible tune: WESTMINSTER ABBEY
Topics: Love, Prayer, Service, Witnessing, Youth

God of Eagles, God of Sparrows

87 87 D

God of eagles, God of sparrows,
soaring spirit, earthly guide,
help our nation know true greatness,
free from all-consuming pride.
Strengthen us for global duties
sharing progress that is just;
like the eagle may we venture,
like the sparrow may we trust.

God of valleys, God of mountains,
comrade in our depths and heights,
speak through all our civic leaders
who would nurture human rights.
May they know your daily presence
and affirm your ageless deeds;
through dark valleys may they follow,
up steep mountains where love leads.

God in victory, God in failure,
steadfast through each tribal test,
save us from our shabby idols,
show us that your way is best.
Better than the lure of power,
better than the lust for fame;
so in failure may we praise you,
and in victory bless your name.

Words: Dosia Carlson (b. 1930)
Source: "New Hymns for America: 1976," 1975
Possible tune: IN BABILONE
Topics: Creation, Nation, Sovereignty of God

God of Earth and Planets

65 65

God of earth and planets
ranging outer space:
we in silent wonder
glimpse your might and grace.

God of worlds and atoms,
each a masterpiece:
deepest probes of science
awe and faith increase.

God of flower and ocean—
fragrance, beauty, power:
of your love and bounty
share we every hour.

God of home and family,
God our parents know:
in your love and knowledge
we would live and grow.

God who sent us Jesus—
Master, Friend, and Guide:
we would call you "Father,"
in your care abide.

Words: William Watkins Reid, alt. (1890-1983)
Source: "Twelve New Hymns for Children", 1965;
The Hymn 17:113 (October, 1966)
Possible tunes: GOD OF EARTH (*The Hymn*, October 1966),
WEM IN LEIDENSTAGEN (H82 479)
Scriptural references: Matthew 6:9, Luke 11:2
Topics: Children, Creation, Home and Family, Sovereignty of God

God of the Fertile Fields

664 6664

God of the fertile fields,
Lord of the earth that yields
our daily bread;
forth from thy bounteous hand
come gifts thy love has planned,
that all in every land
be clothed and fed.

We would thy stewards be,
holding in trust from thee
all thou dost give;
help us in love to share,
teach us like you to care,
that earth may all be fair;
your children live.

As grows the hidden seed
to fruit that serves our need,
thy kingdom grows.
So let our toil be used,
no gift of thine abused,
no humble task refused
thy love bestows.

God of the countryside,
dear to our Lord, who died
to make us one;
we pledge our lives to thee
to serve thee faithfully
till in eternity
our day is done.

Words: Georgia Harkness, 1955 (1891-1974)
Source: "Fourteen New Rural Hymns," 1955;
The Hymn 26:43 (April 1975)
Possible tunes: ITALIAN HYMN, MILTON ABBAS (HWB)
Topics: Earth, Ecology/Environment, Forgiveness,
Rural Life, Stewardship

God, the Lord of Lowly Places

87 87 87

God, the Lord of lowly places,
speak to us in common things,
thou through whom a manger cradle
joined the shepherds with the kings.
Make us humble; make us faithful,
guide for all our journeyings.

God, the Lord of help and healing,
send us out to work for thee;
like thy Son, the great physician,
let each one thy servant be.
Make us humble; make us faithful;
bless our toil abundantly.

God, the Lord of prayerful living,
gird us for the task begun,
as of old upon the mountain
thou didst strengthen Christ thy Son.
Make us humble; make us faithful,
striving that thy will be done.

Lord our God, on high exalted,
lift our souls thy grace to prove;
thou didst turn the cross to triumph;
draw us by thy perfect love.
Make us humble; make us faithful,
one in Christ with hosts above.

Words: Jane O. Thurber, alt. (b. 1930)
Source: "Five New Hymns for Youth by Youth," 1955
Possible tune: PICARDY
Topics: Faithfulness, Healing, Humility, Image of God, Prayer, Youth

God, Who Gave Us Life and Beauty*

85 85

God, who gave us life and beauty,
  help us realize
how you blessed us with your gift of
  lands and seas and skies.

You who gave us crystal waters,
  golden sunshine's light,
help us keep them as you gave them:
  clear and pure and bright.

Help us know when we defile them,
  we dishonor you;
and in caring, we preserve them,
  we are thanking you.

*Original first line: God who gave us all this beauty

Words: Frances E. Weir, alt. (b. 1912)
Source: "16 New Hymns on Stewardship of the Environment," 1973; *The Hymn* 24:87 (July 1973)
Possible tunes: SPIRITUS CHRISTE (HB 243)
Topics: Gratitude, Stewardship

God, Whose Giving Knows No Ending

87 87 D

God, whose giving knows no ending,
  from your rich and endless store:
nature's wonder, Jesus' wisdom,
  costly cross, grave's shattered door,
gifted by you, we turn to you,
  offering up ourselves in praise;
thankful song shall rise forever,
  gracious donor of our days.

Skills and time are ours for pressing
  toward the goals of Christ, your Son:
all at peace in health and freedom,
  races joined, the Church made one.
Now direct our daily labor,
  lest we strive for self alone;
born with talents, make us servants
  fit to answer at your throne.

Treasure, too, you have entrusted,
  gain through powers your grace conferred;
ours to use for home and kindred,
  and to spread the Gospel word.
Open wide our hands in sharing,
  as we heed Christ's ageless call,
healing, teaching, and reclaiming,
  serving you by loving all.

Words: Robert L. Edwards, alt. (b. 1915)
Source: "Ten New Stewardship Hymns," 1961
Possible tunes: RUSTINGTON, BEACH SPRING, HYFRYDOL
Scriptural references: Philippians 3:14, Philippians 4:19
Topics: Gratitude, Service/Servanthood, Stewardship

Good News for This New Age

66 66 88

Good news for this new age
our song of Christmas brings;
around this troubled world
God's word of healing rings.
  Sing joy, sing peace, sing freedom, life,
  for Christ is born to end our strife.

A Child is born to save
from sorrow, pain, and sin:
for all in evil's power
their human rights to win.
  Sing joy, sing peace, sing freedom, life,
  for Christ is born to end our strife.

The Prince of Peace is born
that we, with God at one,
may serve all humankind,
and all God's will be done.
  Sing joy, sing peace, sing freedom, life,
  for Christ is born to end our strife.

To Bethlehem, then, come,
your infant Lord lies here;
with worship, gifts, and love,
to honor him draw near.
  Sing joy, sing peace, sing freedom, life,
  for Christ is born to end our strife.

Words: Albert F. Bayly, alt. (1901-1984)
Source: *The Hymn* 22:116 (October 1971)
Possible tune: DARWALL'S 148TH
Topics: Christmas, Freedom, Peace, Salvation

Great God, We Lift Our Hearts

87 87 66 66 7

Great God, we lift our hearts in praise
for blessings without measure.
We give you thanks for length of days,
and hold your time as treasure.
In years that still remain
make subject to your reign
each passing day and hour.
Sustain us in your power,
for you are God eternal!

Though endless ages in your sight
are moments quickly fading,
your care surrounds each day and night
all time and space pervading.
The past your mercy holds.
Your love this day unfolds,
and for each future care
your wisdom will be there,
for you are God eternal!

O Ever-Ancient, Ever-New,
creation chants your story.
Unfolding worlds return to you
their hymn of praise and glory.
So may our lives proclaim
the glory of your name,
as human plans unfold
within your plan of old,
for you are God eternal!

Words: Miriam Therese Putzer
Source: *The Hymn* 38:34 (January 1987)
Possible tune: EIN FESTE BURG
Scriptural references: Psalm 90:4, II Peter 3:8
Topics: Adoration and Praise, Blessing, New Year/Old Year

Guide Us, O God, in Paths of Truth

CMD

Guide us, O God, in paths of truth
 that lead us to new ways.
Renew our faith, redeem our lives,
 in this new living day.
Give us a sense of righteousness
 born in humility;
help us relate to all of life,
 and find fresh dignity.

Give us the minds that understand
 what human life can be.
Give us the courage in ourselves
 to serve humanity.
To be concerned for human need,
 to live more fruitfully,
help us, O God of trusting love,
 to make each other free.

May each another seek and find
 and share the deepest self.
May each to adversary be
 an instrument of help.
O God of truth, O God of grace,
 lift us to new designs,
until among us shall be found
 a loving humankind.

Words: Gilbert Taverner (b. 1920)
Source: *The Hymn* 27:6 (January 1976)
Possible tune: KINGSFOLD
Scriptural reference: Psalm 25:4-5
Topics: Courage, Prayer, Service, Truth

Help Us, O Lord, to Learn

SM

Help us, O Lord, to learn
the truths your word imparts;
to study, that your laws may be
inscribed upon our hearts.

Help us, O Lord, to live
the faith which we proclaim,
that all our thoughts and words and deeds
may glorify your name.

Help us, O Lord, to teach
the beauty of your ways,
that yearning souls may find the Christ
and sing aloud his praise.

Words: William W. Reid, Jr., alt. (b. 1923)
Source: "Fifteen New Christian Education Hymns," 1959
Possible tune: ST. THOMAS
Scriptural references: Deuteronomy 6:6, Psalm 119:11
Topics: Christian Nurture/ Education, Jesus Christ, Word of God

Hope of the World

11 10 11 10

Hope of the world, thou Christ of great compassion,
  speak to our fearful hearts by conflict rent.
Save us, thy people, from consuming passion,
  who by our own false hopes and aims are spent.

Hope of the world, God's gift from highest heaven,
  bringing to hungry souls the bread of life,
still let thy Spirit unto us be given
  to heal earth's wounds and end all bitter strife.

Hope of the world, afoot on dusty highways,
  showing to wandering souls the path of light;
walk thou beside us lest the tempting byways
  lure us away from thee to endless night.

Hope of the world, who by thy cross did save us
  from death and dark despair, from sin and guilt;
we render back the love thy mercy gave us;
  take thou our lives and use them as thou wilt.

Hope of the world, O Christ, o'er death victorious,
  who by this sign didst conquer grief and pain,
we would be faithful to thy gospel glorious:
  Thou art our Lord! Thou dost forever reign!

Words: Georgia Harkness, alt. (1891-1974)
Source: "Eleven Ecumencial Hymns," 1954
Possible tunes: GENEVAN 12 (DONNE SECOURS),
  SPES MUNDI (see p. 164), VICAR
Topics: Ecumenism, Hope, Jesus Christ, Life in Christ,
  Ministry, Mission

How Blest Are They Who Trust in Christ

LM

How blest are they who trust in Christ
when we and those we love must part;
we yield them up, for go we must,
but do not lose them from our heart.

In ripened age, their harvest reaped,
or gone from us in youth or prime,
in Christ they have eternal life,
released from all the bonds of time.

In Christ, who tasted death for us,
we rise above our natural grief,
and witness to a stricken world
the strength and splendor of belief.

Words: Fred Pratt Green (b. 1903)
Source: *The Hymn* 32:49 (January 1981)
Possible tunes: ROCKINGHAM, CANONBURY, MARYTON
Scriptural reference: Hebrews 2:9
Topics: Funeral/Memorial Service, Trust

In the Beginning, Before Pain and Sinning

569 669

In the beginning,
before pain and sinning,
the Lord of life made everything good;
but we disobeyed him,
rejected, betrayed him,
so God sent Christ, the Life of the world!

Eyes never seeing,
from truth always fleeing,
now saw the Lord bring sight to the blind;
and deaf ears, unhearing
until his appearing,
were healed by Christ, the Life of the world!

Darkness can cover
the universe over;
injustice, sin, and violence prevail;
Yet God's Spirit moves us
to tell how God loves us,
proclaiming Christ, the Life of the world!

Each son and daughter,
in bread, wine, and water,
may claim the Father's grace through the Son;
and when the grave takes us
our faith in God makes us
alive in Christ, the Life of the world!

Nothing can please us
without life in Jesus,
to him we're joined as fruit to the vine;
the Spirit invites us,
the Father unites us,
made one in Christ, the Life of the world!

Words: Rae E. Whitney (b. 1927)
Source: *The Hymn* 34:158(July 1983)
Possible tune: LIFE OF THE WORLD (see p. 138)
Scriptural references: Genesis 1:28, Genesis 1:31, John 15:1-8
Topics: Communion, Holy Spirit/Pentecost, Unity

In the Beginning, Lord

66 84 D

In the beginning, Lord,
you made the world in love;
you made us stewards of the earth
  and skies above!
You placed the ocean deeps,
the riches of the land,
the rushing rivers, shining hills
  into our hand!

The centuries have passed,
but now we see it's true:
we used these riches for ourselves,
  forgetting you!
Behold the barren hills,
the smog against the sun,
imprisoned rivers, dying seas—
  what have we done?

We are ashamed to see
earth's riches sadly spent.
Our stewardship we have betrayed,
  and we repent!
Lord, help us now restore
this world which you have made,
and give us strength that this great task
  be not delayed!

Words: Judith Woodward, alt.
Source: "Sixteen New Hymns on the Stewardship of the Environment," 1973
Possible tune: LEONI
Scriptural reference: Psalm 8:6-8
Topics: Confession, Ecology/Environment, Stewardship

Isaiah the Prophet Has Written of Old

Irregular

Isaiah the prophet has written of old
  how God's earthly kingdom shall come.
Instead of the thorn tree the fir tree shall grow;
  the wolf shall lie down with the lamb.
The mountains and hills shall break forth into song,
  the peoples be led forth in peace;
for the earth shall be filled with the knowledge of God
  as the waters cover the seas.

Yet nations still prey on the meek of the world,
  and conflict turns parent from child.
Your people despoil all the sweetness of earth;
  the briar and the thorn grow wild.
Lord, hasten to bring in your kingdom on earth,
  when no one shall hurt or destroy,
when wisdom and justice shall reign in the land
  and your people shall go forth in joy.

Words: Joy F. Patterson, 1982 (b. 1932)
Source: "New Hymns for Children," 1982
Possible tune: SAMANTHRA (PsH 616, PH 337)
Scriptural references: Isaiah 11:6-9, Isaiah 55:12-13
Topics: Advent, Justice, Peace, Word of God

Jesus, Life of All the World

78 78 77

Jesus, life of all the world,
source and sum of all creation,
Son of God and Son of Man,
only hope of our salvation,
    living Word for all our need,
    life you give is life indeed!

Life of freedom, gladness, truth,
all our guilt and fear transcending;
life that leaps beyond the grave,
God's own life that knows no ending;
    life eternal, gift unpriced,
    freely ours in Jesus Christ!

Yours is life that makes us stand
firm for truth, all wrong defying;
yours the strength by which we strive,
on your holy arm relying;
    yours the war we wage on sin,
    yours the power by which we win.

Jesus, life of all the world,
you are Lord of every nation;
by your Holy Spirit's power
make your Church your incarnation
    till our lives of truth and grace
    show the world your human face!

Words: Margaret Clarkson (b. 1915)
Source: *The Hymn* 34:157 (July 1983)
Possible tune: JESU, MEINE ZUVERSICHT
Scriptural references: John 10:10, Romans 6:23
Topics: Incarnation, Jesus Christ

Lead Me from Death to Life

SM

Lead me from death to life,
from falsehood into truth;
and may I keep, through all my years,
the wondrous joy of youth.

From dark despair to hope,
from fear to trust in God,
from hate to love, from war to peace,
keep leading me, dear Lord.

Let peace enfold my heart;
in peace my soul immerse;
and may God's peace pervade the world,
then fill the universe!

Words: Rae E. Whitney (b. 1927)
Source: *The Hymn* 36:21 (July 1985)
Possible tunes: CARLISLE,
PAX IN TERRA (*The Hymn*, July 1985)
Topics: Eternal Life, Peace, Truth

Let Heaven Rejoice Before the Living Lord

10 10 10 10

Let heaven rejoice before the living Lord;
let earth resound where'er his voice is heard;
let all creation join the hymn of praise:
"Great is our God in all his works and ways."

Let surging oceans lend their mighty voice;
let soaring birds and flowing streams rejoice;
let lofty mountain peaks and sighing trees
make known their praise to every passing breeze.

O God, your beauty everywhere is seen
in winter snow and summer's robe of green,
in Word made flesh, Christ with us here to stay,
in lives made holy as they find your way.

Let angel choirs and saints their anthems raise;
let all creation sing its song of praise:
to Father, Son, and Spirit, One in Three,
be glory now and to eternity.

Words: Hal M. Helms (b. 1923)
Source: *The Hymn* 38:32 (January 1987)
Possible tune: ROCK HARBOR (see p. 154)
Scriptural references: Psalm 96:11-12, Psalm 98:7-8, John 1:14,
Revelation 15:3
Topics: Adoration and Praise, Creation

Let the Songs of Earth Arise

77 77 D

Let the songs of earth arise,
mounting upward to the skies,
voices joined in grateful praise
for the love that crowns our days.
Long ago the stars of light
pierced the darkness of the night,
heard the angel voice proclaim
glory to God's holy name.

Sages watching eastern skies
saw a greater star arise;
gathered gifts and made their way
to a child amid the hay;
found God's glory come to earth
in the miracle of birth,
in a father's strong embrace,
in a mother's shining face.

Shepherds in the fields at night
found their darkness turned to light;
heard angelic voices sing
of a more than earthly king;
one whose love would rule the earth
through the gift of second birth
and the reign of peace extend
unto earth's remotest end.

Still today we see the star,
worshipers from near and far;
still we hear the angels' song
though the night be dark and long.
Ever in our hearts a voice
sounds the summons to rejoice;
calls us to a life of praise
for the love that crowns our days.

Words: Edwin O. Kennedy, 1976, alt. (b. 1900)
Source: *The Hymn* 35:45 (January 1984)
Possible tune: ST. GEORGE'S WINDSOR
Scriptural references: Matthew 2:1-12, Luke 2:8-15
Topics: Epiphany, Light, Love

Lift up Your Eyes

11 10 11 10

Lift up your eyes! The dawn you seek is bending
to bless our night with fingers of the day;
the bonds of darkness Christ the Light is rending;
Lo! where he comes old terrors flee away.

Lift up your hands! By love your Christ is broken,
the Bread of Life for all earth's hungry throngs;
the table spread, your presence long forespoken,
feast here in peace, for here the world belongs.

Lift up your hearts! Obey your risen Master;
grant him abode; and he will dwell with you
and give you back rejoicing for disaster,
beauty for dust, and all the world made new.

Lift up your souls! Possess your full salvation;
on you the Savior's pardon has been poured;
you are the heirs of ancient expectation;
yours is the shining kingdom of the Lord.

Words: John Underwood Stephens, alt. (b. 1901)
Source: "Eleven Ecumenical Hymns," 1954
Possible tune: DONNE SECOURS
Topics: Advent, Ecumenism, Light, Salvation

Lord, As You Taught Us Once to Pray

88 88 88 88 88

Lord, as you taught us once to pray,
so teach us now in love to live.
You showed the world the better way,
you sought us lost and fugitive.
You changed our wills from "must" to "may,"
you calm us with your "I forgive,"
and all our fears are soothed away.
It is by love that we survive.
Lord, as you taught us once to pray,
so teach us now in love to live.

As you for love were crucified,
so teach us, Lord, that way to peace.
You healed the hurts of those who cried,
you made the griefs of mourners cease,
gave Satan's prey a place to hide.
Who sees you on your cross-bound knees,
sees love that cannot be denied.
This kind of love in us increase.
As you for love were crucified,
so teach us, Lord, that way to peace.

As you obeyed your Father's plan,
make us such vessels of your grace.
We need no other reason than
that we reflect our Father's face.
Show us the depth and height and span
of love that spares no sacrifice,
and we shall do what you began:
reach to the world with your embrace.
As you obeyed your Father's plan,
make us such vessels of your grace.

Lord, as in love you saw God's will,
so make that love, that will, ours too.
This world in endless dryness still
will die and dies without your dew.
Since God is love, and angels thrill
to find this wonder ever new,
his gracious will help us fulfill
and join his joyful retinue.
Lord, as in love you saw God's will,
so make that love, that will, ours too.

Words: Jaroslav J. Vajda (b. 1919)
Source: "Three Hymns for 1979," 1979
Possible tune: ANNIE LYTLE (see p. 119)
Scriptural reference: I John 4:8
Topics: Guidance, Lent, Love, Peace, Prayer

Lord, at Your Table Kneeling

777 4

Lord, at your table kneeling,
our deepest needs revealing,
we turn to you appealing,
show us your love!

A loaf of bread is broken
as words of truth are spoken,
and faith receives a token,
Lord, of your love.

Lord, from your cup receiving,
no darkness now deceiving,
we look to you believing;
thank you for love!

Now from your table rising,
we go with joy surprising;
in each new task, arising
to share your love.

Words: William W. Reid, Jr., alt. (b. 1923)
Source: "New Hymns, Songs, and Prayers for Church and Home," 1974
Possible tune: MEYER (RL 379)
Topics: Communion, Home and Family, Love, Prayer

Lord of Nations, God Eternal

87 87 D

Lord of nations, God Eternal,
lift we songs of praise to thee,
for our nation strong and mighty;
may thy blessings ever be
on our land, a land of beauty,
land of freedom, land we love;
fields and valleys, plains and mountains,
spreading 'neath blue skies above.

Make our nation strong in justice,
that the people still shall know
freedom from all fear and danger
from within, from outward foe.
O renew us in true valor,
that like founders of this land,
we may stand for right and honor,
seeking guidance by thy hand.

Turn our eyes to things eternal,
let us learn the truth anew:
that we never find salvation
by the things that we can do.
Teach us that we are but pilgrims
as our ancestors before;
that we journey here a season,
trav'ling to an unknown shore.

Fill our hearts with hope and courage,
let us sing the songs of peace,
as in common love we labor
that true justice may increase.
Give us hearts that know compassion,
helping others on their way;
till all people live in freedom,
and accept thy sovereign sway.

Words: H. Glen Lanier, alt. (1925-1978)
Source: "New Hymns for America," 1976
Possible tune: HYMN TO JOY
Topics: Freedom, Nation

Lord, We Bring to You Our Children

87 87

Lord, we bring to you our children
 on this festive, holy day.
Grant to them your benediction;
 grant to us your help, we pray.

Now may we in honest worship,
 in this glad and sacred hour,
give ourselves in true commitment
 to your service and your power;

to the task of Christian nurture:
 teaching, training, leading still
in the way of Christ-like living
 till life's purpose we fulfill.

Bless the children! Bless the parents!
 May they grow in Christ our Lord:
joined in faith and loving service,
 in his Spirit and his word.

Words: Frank von Christierson, 1974 (b. 1900)
Source: "New Hymns, Songs, and Prayers for Church and Home," 1974
Possible tunes: STUTTGART, WYCLIFF (WC 759)
Topics: Baptism/Consecration, Christian Nurture/Education, Commitment

Lord, We Give Humble Thanks Today

LM

Lord, we give humble thanks today
for bounties strewn along our way,
for gifts that have made manifest
how very richly we are blest;

for creatures of the field and wood
who share our love, for ill or good,
the clear frog chorus in the spring,
the sudden flash of bluebird wing;

for undulating, golden grain
upon the rolling, patterned plain,
and orchard trees whose boughs are bent
with summer's jewels freely lent;

for brilliant hues of tapestries
of shrub and vine and flaming trees
when birch and sumac burn and glow
before the hush of winter's snow.

The life, the land, the sea, the air
have been entrusted to our care;
we pray, O Lord, that we may be
good stewards of this earth for thee.

Words: Julia E. Brigham and Pauline E. Kennedy, alt.
Source: "Sixteen New Hymns on the Stewardship of the Environment," 1973
Possible tune: GERMANY
Scriptural references: Genesis 1:28, Psalm 8:6-8
Topics: Creation, Ecology/Environment, Gratitude, Stewardship

Lord, When I Stand, No Path Before Me Clear

10 10 10 10

Lord, when I stand, no path before me clear,
when every prayer seems prisoner of my pain,
come with a gentleness which calms my fear;
Lord of my helplessness, my victory gain.

When all my prayers no answer seem to bring,
and there is silence in my deepest soul,
when in the wilderness I find no spring,
Lord of the desert places, keep me whole.

When the dark lord of loneliness prevails,
and, all defeated, joy and friendship die,
come, be my joy, such love that never fails;
pierce the self pity of my shadowed sky.

When as did Thomas I presume thee dead,
feeling and faith itself within me cold,
freshen my lips with wine, my soul with bread,
banish my poverty with heaven's gold.

Words: Herbert O'Driscoll, 1980 (b. 1928)
Source: *The Hymn* 32:242 (October 1981)
Possible tune: LANGRAN (PsH 74)
Scriptural reference: John 20:24-25
Topics: Guidance, Lent, Prayer, Saints

Lord, You Have Given Your Church for Its Healing*

11 10 11 10

Lord, you have given your Church for its healing
gifts, and the grace to sustain and renew.
Hear as we pray that today and tomorrow
we to your purpose may show ourselves true.

Clear be the voices of preachers and prophets
fearlessly speaking the word of the Lord,
word of redemption through God's Son incarnate,
blessing for cursing and peace for the sword.

Tender and wise be the hearts of the pastors,
guiding and guarding the souls in their care,
firm with the wayward, a strength to the doubting,
helping the needy their burdens to bear.

May those who teach grow in knowledge and patience,
guiding to wisdom the young and the old,
training for worship and witness and service,
foe to all falsehood, in truthfulness bold.

Lord, ever give to us gifts in due measure,
each needing others and all having worth.
Praise to the Father, the Son, and the Spirit;
glory be shown by the Church here on earth.

*Original first line: Lord, who dost give to thy church for its healing

Words: Ernest A. Payne, alt. (1902-1980)
Source: "Ten New Hymns on the Ministry," 1966
Possible tune: O QUANTA QUALIA
Topics: Christian Nurture/Education, Church, Gifts, Healing, Ministry

Loving Spirit

87 87

Loving Spirit, loving Spirit,
you have chosen me to be —
you have drawn me to your wonder,
you have set your sign on me.

Like a mother, you enfold me,
hold my life within your own,
feed me with your very body,
form me of your flesh and bone.

Like a father, you protect me,
teach me the discerning eye,
hoist me up upon your shoulder,
let me see the world from high.

Friend and lover, in your closeness
I am known and held and blessed;
in your promise is my comfort,
in your presence I may rest.

Loving Spirit, loving Spirit,
you have chosen me to be —
you have drawn me to your wonder,
you have set your sign on me.

Words: Shirley Erena Murray, 1989 (b. 1931)
Source: *The Hymn* 41:33 (April 1990)
Possible tunes: OMNI DIE (PH 323), STUTTGART
Topics: Holy Spirit, Image of God, Presence of God

Make Us, O God, a Church That Shares

CMD

Make us, O God, a church that shares
your love for humankind;
that lives the truth your word declares,
and heeds the Master's mind.
Help us reach out with loving hands,
in times that try the soul,
with sympathy that understands
and makes the needy whole.

Make us, O God, a church that cares
for every human need;
that suffers when one life despairs,
and moves to intercede.
Give to our voice prophetic power
that stirs each wavering heart
to meet the challenge of this hour
and take a noble part.

Make us, O God, a church that dares
courageously to act;
that clothes with flesh its fervent prayers
and makes the gospel fact.
Now thrust us from the cloistered halls
where fearful souls might hide,
and send us forth where duty calls
to serve the Crucified!

Words: H. Victor Kane, alt.
Source: *The Hymn* 22:4 (October 1971)
Possible tune: ALL SAINTS
Topics: Church, Prayer, Service/Servanthood

Mountain Brook with Rushing Waters

87 87 D

Mountain brook with rushing waters,
eagle perched in lofty tree,
flowering hillside in the springtime,
white-tailed deer alert and free!
Beauty, beauty all around us!
Jubilate! Sing for joy!
Help us, God, preserve earth's splendor
for tomorrow's world to see.

Pure the water freshly flowing
toward its ocean-destiny,
clean the air of God's creation,
rich the soil, the mine, the sea.
"Earth is good!" God's word proclaimed it.
Jubilate! Sing for joy!
Save us, God, from wasteful living,
from pollution's tragedy.

Waving fields of wheat and barley,
giant apples—juicy red,
cattle grazing in the pasture;
by God's bounty we are fed!
Well-supplied the world around us!
Jubilate! Sing for joy!
May no greed or warring madness
scorch the earth or rob our bread.

Keep us faithful in the struggle
to conserve earth's threatened store,
as we fight to save the forest,
clean the stream, protect the shore.
God and humans work together.
Jubilate! Sing for joy!
Partners working till as stewards
we can say "Earth's good!" once more.

Words: William W. Reid, Jr. (b. 1923)
Source: "Sixteen New Hymns on Stewardship
of the Environment," 1973
Possible tunes: HOLY MANNA, MOUNTAIN BROOK (see p. 140)
Scriptural reference: Genesis 1:31
Topics: Creation, Ecology/Environment, Stewardship

O Christ, Whose Love Has Sought Us Out

LM

O Christ, whose love has sought us out,
alone and lost in desert ways;
we gather round your cross again
in wonder and united praise.

Your life is still the miracle,
our way of living far above,
beyond the reaches of our minds.
We cannot understand; we love.

Ancestral gifts within our hands,
the cherished treasures from the past,
we lay before your feet, O Lord:
cleanse, use them, make them yours at last.

So may we all be one in you,
whose revelations never cease,
whose love and truth are ever new,
and in whose service is our peace.

Words: John Edgar Park, 1953, alt. (1880-1956)
Source: "Eleven Ecumenical Hymns," 1954
Possible tune: TRURO
Topics: Ecumenism, Jesus Christ, Lent, Offering

O Church of God, United

76 76 D

O Church of God, united
to serve one common Lord,
proclaim to all one message,
with hearts in glad accord.
Christ ever goes before us;
we follow day by day
with strong and eager footsteps
along the upward way.

From every land and nation
the ordered ranks appear;
to serve one valiant leader
they come from far and near.
They chant their one confession,
they praise one living Lord,
and place their sure dependence
upon his saving word.

Though creeds and tongues may differ,
they speak, O Christ, of thee;
and in thy loving spirit,
we shall one people be.
Lord, may our faithful service
and singleness of aim
proclaim to all the power
of thy redeeming name.

May thy great prayer be answered
that we may all be one,
close bound, by love united
in thee, God's blessed Son:
to bring a single witness,
to make the pathway bright,
that souls which grope in darkness
may find the one true light.

Words: Frederick B. Morley, 1953 (1894-1979)
Source: "Eleven Ecumenical Hymns," 1954
Possible tunes: MUNICH, LANCASHIRE
Scriptural reference: John 17:20-23
Topics: Church, Ecumenism, Unity, Witnessing

O Father, Son, and Holy Spirit, Hear

10 10 10 10

O Father, Son, and Holy Spirit, hear;
thou who dost know our doubting and our grief,
grant the petition of each heart sincere:
"Lord, I believe; help thou mine unbelief."

Should faith in Christ's redemption fall away;
and fear devour, and doubt come like a thief
to steal our peace and joy, help each to pray:
"Lord, I believe; help thou mine unbelief."

Our Father, from pride's bondage set us free,
since anyone of sinners might be chief;
our souls make humble till we cry to thee:
"Lord, I believe; help thou mine unbelief."

Dear Son of God, who in Gethsemane
didst bear our burdens, finding no relief,
destroy temptation's power and hear each plea:
"Lord, I believe; help thou mine unbelief."

O Holy Spirit, grace bestow that we
may grow in faith, though years of life be brief—
till faith shall lead to sight, our prayer shall be:
"Lord, I believe; help thou mine unbelief."

Words: James Boeringer, 1957, alt. (b.1930)
Source: *The Hymn* 10:64 (April 1959)
Possible tune: COKE–JEPHCOTT (see p. 124)
Scriptural reference: Mark 9:24
Topics: Faith, Lent, Prayer, Trinity

O God in Heaven

88 88 88 or LM with Refrain

O God in heaven, whose loving plan
ordained for us our parents' care,
and from the time our life began,
the shelter of a home to share.
    Refrain:
    Our Father, on the homes we love
    send down your blessing from above.

May young and old together find
in Christ, the Lord of every day,
that fellowship our homes may bind
in joy and sorrow, work and play.
    Refrain

Forgive the sins that mar our lives;
our selfishness by love subdue;
as parents, children, make us wise
in glad obedience to you.
    Refrain

O Father, in our home preside,
there duties shared as in your sight;
in kindly ways be now our guide,
on mirth and trouble shed your light.
    Refrain

Words: Hugh Martin, alt.
Source: "Thirteen New Marriage and Family Life Hymns," 1961
Possible tune: LEICESTER (PsH 139)
Topics: Home and Family, Weddings/Christian Marriage

O God of Every Nation

76 76 D

O God of every nation,
    of every race and land,
redeem the whole creation
    with your almighty hand.
Where hate and fear divide us
    and bitter threats are hurled,
in love and mercy guide us,
    and heal our strife-torn world.

From search for wealth and power
    and scorn of truth and right,
from trust in bombs that shower
    destruction through the night,
from pride of race and station
    and blindness to your way,
deliver every nation,
    eternal God, we pray!

Lord, strengthen all who labor
    that we may find release
from fear of rattling saber,
    from dread of war's increase.
When hope and courage falter,
    Lord, let your voice be heard;
with faith that none can alter,
    your servants undergird.

Keep bright in us the vision
    of days when war shall cease,
when hatred and division
    give way to love and peace,
till dawns the morning glorious
    when truth and justice reign,
and Christ shall rule victorious
    o'er all the world's domain.

Words: William W. Reid, Jr., 1958, alt. (b. 1923)
Source: "Twelve New World Order Hymns," 1958
Possible tune: LLANGLOFFAN
Topics: International Life, Justice, Kingdom of God, Peace,
    Social Concerns/Welfare, Sovereignty of God, World Order

O God of Heaven, We Give Thee Thanks

CMD

O God of heaven, we give thee thanks
 for all thy gifts of light:
the brilliance of the sun by day,
 the moon and stars by night;
and that most gracious Light of lights,
 our Savior and our King,
who came the night of sin to end,
 eternal day to bring.

O God of earth, we give thee thanks
 for making earth so fair;
for plains and mountains, lakes and streams,
 for sky and sea and air.
O God of life, we give thee thanks
 for grass and herb and tree,
for living creatures of all kinds,
 and for humanity.

O God, who marks the sparrow's fall,
 teach us to treat this earth
and all its life with tender care,
 for thou didst give it birth,
and thou didst interweave its parts
 into a fragile whole
that ignorance and greed can wreck:
 make stewardship our goal.

O Day Star, end our night of sin,
 our plundering of the earth,
our savagery to living things.
 Teach us to know the worth
of all thy gifts, and to accept
 them as a trust from thee.
Help us to guard them for all time
 and for eternity.

Words: Anastasia van Burkalow, alt. (b. 1911)
Source: "Sixteen New Hymns on Stewardship of the Environment," 1973
Possible tune: ALL SAINTS NEW
Topics: Ecology/Environment, Gratitude, Light, Stewardship

O God of Love, Who Gavest Life

CM

O God of love, who gavest life,
what shall we give to thee,
whose wealth is all the universe,
whose time eternity?

Take thou, O Lord, our humble hearts,
devoted to thy praise,
our very selves—in gratitude
to serve thee all our days.

Thus we would give our precious time,
each dedicated hour
to be an offering blest of thee
to make thy church a power.

And all the talents that we have
we pray thee use, O Lord,
to magnify thy glorious name
and spread abroad thy word.

So then with heart and time and skills
all given in love to thee,
we gladly share our earthly goods
to bless humanity.

Words: E. Urner Goodman (b. 1891)
Source: "Ten New Stewardship Hymns," 1961
Possible tune: WINCHESTER OLD
Topics: Adoration and Praise, Gifts, Offering, Stewardship

O God of Youth, We Come to You for Leading

11 10 11 10

O God of youth, we come to you for leading,
our minds to guide, our spirits to set free;
we search for truth and love, your statutes heeding,
give us, O Lord, a sense of destiny.

The stress is great and absolutes are bending.
We cannot find our way without your care;
it seems the search goes ever forth unending,
and fainting hearts cry out, "O Master, where?"

O God of youth, come near and speak your blessing;
give us a sense of what is worthy, true.
We come to you, our helplessness confessing,
and cannot rest until we rest in you.

Words: Carlton C. Buck (b. 1907)
Source: "Ten New Hymns for the 70's," 1970
Possible tunes: DONNE SECOURS, VICAR
Topics: Guidance, Youth

O God, Whose Favor Hallows All Occasions*

11 10 11 10 10 10

O God, whose favor hallows all occasions,
be present at this covenanting rite;
may every pledge of true and lasting purpose
receive approval in your holy sight;
confer on those before you heavenly aid
to keep the solemn vows that here are made.

Long may they keep the sense of high adventure,
the gift of joy, the marvel of a dream,
and never lose the vision as they cherish
each for the other honor and esteem;
enrich them with the blessing of your grace,
and make their home your constant dwelling place.

Almighty God, Redeemer and Defender,
O be their stay whatever may betide;
may each new year increasingly discover
their lives matured, their marriage sanctified,
their hearts firm-fixed on this exalted goal:
the praise of God whose Name their vows extol.

*Original first line: O thou, whose favor hallows all occasions

Words: Miriam Drury, alt. (b. 1900)
Source: "Thirteen New Marriage and Family Life Hymns," 1961
Possible tune: FINLANDIA
Topics: Commitment, Covenant, Weddings/Christian Marriage

O God, Whose Mighty Wisdom Moves

88 88 88

O God, whose mighty wisdom moves
our human minds to seek thy way,
by thee our forebears sought the law;
Lord, keep us in that quest today,
that in thy light we yet may see
the path that leads through truth to thee.

O God, whose perfect holiness
inspires our search to find thy will,
by thee the prophets spoke of old;
Lord, let us hear them speaking still,
that in thy light we yet may see
the path that leads through right to thee.

O God, whose tender, yearning heart
gave us a Son, the living Word,
by thee the Good News was sent forth;
Lord, let this Gospel now be heard,
that in thy light we yet may see
the path that leads through love to thee.

O God, whose surging Spirit stirs
within the souls of all on earth,
by thee the Scriptures bring new life,
and hopes forgotten find rebirth.
Lord, grant us in thy light to see
the path that leads through life to thee.

Words: George Brandon, 1952, alt. (b. 1924)
Source: *The Hymn* 7:35 (January 1956)
Possible tune: MELITA
Scriptural reference: Psalm 36:9
Topics: Holy Spirit, Trinity, Wisdom, Word of God

O God, Wise Creator, Sustainer, and Guide

11 11 11 11

O God, wise Creator, Sustainer, and Guide
of planets, of nations, of continents wide:
we thank you for blessings your bounty bestowed
on lands that the poor chose for freedom's abode.

We thank you for prairies, for mountains, for seas,
for wealth of your grain, for the fruit of your trees.
We thank you, O God, for abundance to share
so no child may hunger, no mother despair.

With fruits of your Spirit in our wakened soul,
with fruits of your science revealing our goal,
with saints and with prophets to lead us your way,
we thank you, O God, for new visions today.

Upon this fair land, and upon every land,
may blessings be shared from your generous hand,
till nations and races proclaim you their Lord,
and Earth, your new Eden, shall banish the sword.

Words: Benjamin Caufield, alt.
Source: *The Hymn* 26:29 (January 1975)
Possible tunes: FOUNDATION, ST. DENIO
Topics: Creation, Gratitude

O God, You Made This Wondrous World*

CMD

O God, you made this wondrous world,
  its land and sea and air,
with all that live and grow herein;
  you placed them in our care.
Recipients of your bounty, Lord,
  by luxury beguiled,
O may we not stand idly by
  and see your world defiled.

While all earth's bounteous riches, Lord,
  supply our every need,
let not our fellow creatures fall
  the victims of our greed.
Forbid that we despoil your gifts
  unmindful of the cost,
lest through our wanton wastefulness
  both they and we be lost.

May love control our work on earth,
  enabling its great power
to bring your grand creation, Lord,
  from bud to perfect flower.
May we accept our stewardship
  with humble, thankful hearts,
with diligence and wisdom which
  your grace alone imparts.

*Original first line: O God who made this wondrous world

Words: Florence Emily Cain, alt. (1881-1973)
Source: "16 New Hymns of Stewardship of the Environment," 1973
Possible tune: KINGSFOLD
Topics: Creation, Ecology/Environment, Stewardship

O God, Your Constant Care and Love

LM

O God, your constant care and love
are shed upon us from above,
throughout our lives in every stage,
from infancy to later age.

We thank you, Lord, for dreams of youth,
for wisdom leading on to truth,
for memories gathered through the years,
and faith that grows from joys and tears.

All time is yours, O Lord, to give;
may we, in all the years we live,
find every day of life is new,
a celebration, Lord, with you.

Let not the passing of the years
rob us of joy, nor cause us fears,
and give us faith, O Lord, that we
may live with you, eternally.

Words: H. Glen Lanier, alt. (1925-1978)
Source: "Ten New Hymns on Aging and the Later Years," 1976
Possible tunes: WINCHESTER NEW, WAREHAM
Topics: Aging, Faith, Gratitude, Home and Family, New Year/Old Year

O God, Your Rolling Fields Declare*

CM

O God, your rolling fields declare
the goodness of your hand,
we offer our unbounded thanks
for those who till the land.

For by their hands you do provide
the gift of daily bread;
the throngs who dwell beneath the sun
are by their labors fed.

Reward their earnest toil, O Lord,
with increase of the field;
their hearts inspire to songs of praise
for earth's abundant yield.

Send forth your Spirit unto them
with grace and truth to bless,
and grant to all who seek your face
the fruits of righteousness.

*Original first line: To thee whose rolling fields declare

Words: Frank LeRoy Cross, alt. (b. 1904)
Source: "Fourteen New Rural Hymns," 1955
Possible tune: TALLIS ORDINAL
Topics: Gratitude, Rural Life, Stewardship

O Jesus Christ, May Grateful Hymns Be Rising*

11 10 11 10

O Jesus Christ, may grateful hymns be rising
in every city for your love and care,
inspire our worship, grant the glad surprising
that your blest Spirit rouses everywhere.

Grant us new courage, sacrificial, humble,
strong in your strength to venture and to dare;
to lift the fallen, guide the feet that stumble,
seek out the lonely and God's mercy share.

Show us your Spirit, brooding o'er each city,
as you once wept above Jerusalem,
seeking to gather all in love and pity,
and healing those who touch your garment's hem.

*Original first line: O Jesus Christ, to thee may hymns be rising

Words: Bradford Gray Webster, alt., (b. 1898)
Source: "Five New Hymns of the City," 1954;
The Hymn 19:97 (October 1968)
Possible tunes: CHARTERHOUSE (RL 389), CITY OF GOD (RL 487)
Scriptural references: Luke 8:43-46, Luke 13:34, Luke 19:41
Topics: City, Commitment, Courage, Healing, Holy Spirit,
Jesus Christ, Witnessing, Worship

O Lord, May Church and Home Combine*

CM

O Lord, may church and home combine
to teach thy perfect way,
with gentleness and love like thine,
that none shall ever stray.

Let all unworthy aims depart,
imbue us with thy grace;
within the home let every heart
become thy dwelling place.

Shine, Light divine; reveal thy face
where darkness else might be.
Grant, Love divine, in every place
glad fellowship with thee.

May steadfast faith and earnest prayer
keep sacred vows secure;
build thou a hallowed dwelling where
true joy and peace endure.

*Original first line: Bless thou our Christian homes, O Lord

Words: Carlton C. Buck, 1961, alt. (b. 1907)
Source: "Thirteen New Marriage and Family Life Hymns," 1961
Possible tune: LAND OF REST (UMH 695)
Topics: Christian Nurture/Education, Home and Family, Love

O Lord of Love

11 10 11 10 10 10 10 10

O Lord of love, you once did speak from heaven
to Saul of Tarsus whom all Christians feared,
saying "O Saul, why do you persecute me?
Repent, believe the Father's word revered."
Lord, send us forth from our Damascus road
that we, your church, may proudly name you Lord;
O grant us faith and courage e'er to be
fools for your sake, and guardians of your word.

O Lord of grace, we bless you for the mercies
that touched Paul's heart with beauty and with love;
we cherish all the rich and blessed counsels
that through your Spirit do your presence prove.
Lord, send us forth into the world with grace
that we, your church, may proudly name you Lord;
O grant us faith and courage e'er to be
fools for your sake, and guardians of your word.

O Lord of hope, we celebrate the promise
that heralds now the victory overnight;
O grant us strength to bring about the triumph
of truth and mercy, justice and the right.
Lord, send us forth into the world with joy,
That we, your church, may proudly name you Lord;
O grant us faith and courage e'er to be
fools for your sake, and guardians of your word.

Words: Jackson Hill, alt. (b. 1941)
Source: *The Hymn* 29:175 (July 1978)
Possible tune: ST. PAUL'S, ROCHESTER (see p. 159)
Scriptural references: Acts 9:1-9, II Corinthians 5:13
Topics: Commitment, Faith, Grace, Hope, Love, Saints,
Witnessing, Word of God

O Lord of Love and Power

76 76 D

O Lord of love and power,
your wisdom is the cross;
do save us in the hour
when spirit is at loss.
Our eyes will ever savor
the Christ-child in disguise.
O bless us by your favor;
in weakness make us wise.

O Lord of Word and water,
the sign is on our brow.
The Spirit, Son, and Father
are in our presence now.
In times of joy and sorrow
you made us sure and wise;
so open your tomorrow
as blessing in disguise.

O Lord, we own your story;
your saints have kept us wise.
Your Spirit showed us glory
in lifting up our eyes.
As bread is for the breaking
in sacramental grace,
so love is of your making,
a blessing to our face.

O Lord of now and ages,
of endless stars and sand,
though Satan often rages,
your blessing is at hand.
Our hope is in our holding
Christ Jesus to our eyes;
as blessing keeps unfolding,
surprise us by surprise.

Words: Herbert Brokering (b. 1926)
Source: "Three Hymns for 1979," 1979
Possible tunes: MEIRIONYDD (UMC 436),
SMITH ("Three Hymns for 1979")
Topics: Baptism/Consecration, Blessing, Covenant,
Love, Presence of God

O Lord Our God, Whom All Through Life We Praise

10 10 10 10

O Lord our God, whom all through life we praise,
as year by year days add to numbered days,
with each we prove the wonder of your ways,
while, still adoring, each new song we raise.

With thankful hearts your goodness we confess,
our Guide and Help in gladness and distress.
For life, light, love, your holy name we bless;
accept the gratitude our hearts express.

O God, be near in loneliness and need;
from fear and doubting may our minds be freed.
When losses come, your consolation speed;
for strength and healing love, O Lord, we plead.

Our hope is founded in your saving grace.
Now hope abides to share love every place;
and hope to serve yet spurs our slowing pace,
till, hope fulfilled, we see you face to face.

Words: Frances A. Winters, alt.
Source: "Ten New Hymns on Aging and the Later Years," 1976
Possible tunes: ELLERS, EVENTIDE, TOULON
Scripture reference: I Corinthians 13:11-12
Topics: Adoration and Praise, Aging, Gratitude, Hope

O Lord, the Maze of Earthly Ways

86 86

O Lord, the maze of earthly ways
confuses our intent;
give us thy light to walk aright
through our bewilderment.

The burdened sigh and anguished cry
that so disturb and taunt
are sounds of fear through which we hear
humanity in want.

Give us the heart to do our part,
to live the ancient creed,
express our care, respond, and share,
to meet another's need.

By helping people live again
most fully, we serve thee;
again today we hear thee say,
"You've done it unto me."

Words: Carlton C. Buck, alt. (b. 1907)
Source: "Nine New Hymns on the Mission of the Church," 1969; The *Hymn* 26:91 (July 1975)
Possible tunes: FORLINES (see p. 136), ST. PETER
Scriptural reference: Matthew 25:34-40
Topics: Mission, Service/Servanthood, Social Concerns/Welfare

O Lord, Who Came to Earth to Show

CMD

O Lord, who came to earth to show
 your way of truth and love,
who ministered to varied needs
 with grace sent from above,
equip us now to likewise go,
 and thus fulfill your word
compelling us to minister:
 give us your love, O Lord.

Enable us to hear the cries
 of those who, in despair,
call out for someone who will hear,
 for someone who will care.
Then, hearing, let us actively
 pursue with one accord
a ministry which meets their needs:
 give us your love, O Lord.

With superficial gestures, we
 have tried to comfort those
who struggle for fulfillment in
 the midst of all life's throes.
Invest in us a higher cause
 which, shown by Christ, our Lord,
makes us to seek their deepest needs:
 give us your love, O Lord.

"Your kingdom come on earth," we pray
 with hearts which are resolved,
and yet, in human problems still
 we fail to be involved;
the ministries of comfort, peace,
 and hope may we afford
to all who struggle in their needs:
 give us your love, O Lord.

Words: Milburn Price, alt. (b. 1938)
Source: "Nine New Hymns on the Mission of the Church," 1969
Possible tunes: ELLACOMBE, ALL SAINTS NEW
Scriptural references: Matthew 6:10, Luke 11:2
Topics: Incarnation, Ministry, Mission, Service/Servanthood

O Lord, You Taught Beside the Sea*

86 86 86

O Lord, you taught beside the sea
and on the mountain high,
and in a desert place apart
you prayed with no one nigh;
help us to seek the quiet place
beneath the open sky.

O Lord, your pathway often led
by waves of ripening grain,
to you the lilies of the field
were part of God's domain;
help every eye and mind to see
your beauty once again.

Make us aware of beauty rare
in flower, tree, and sky,
in forests green and fields serene,
in mountains towering high;
but more than all, to hear you call,
and answer, "Here am I."

*Original first line: Thou who didst teach beside the sea

Words: Burton C. Bastuscheck, alt.
Source: "Fourteen New Rural Hymns," 1955
Possible tune: BROTHER JAMES' AIR
Scriptural reference: Isaiah 6:8
Topics: Commitment, Rural Life

O Thou Who Art the Shepherd

76 76 D

O thou who art the Shepherd
of all the scattered sheep,
who lovest all thy lost ones
on every mountain steep,
create in us a yearning
for those whom thou dost seek,
the hopeless and the burdened,
the helpless and the weak.

We would be thy disciples
and all the hungry feed,
nor seek our own salvation
apart from other's need.
These, Father, are thy children
thou sendest us to find;
help us by deeds of mercy
to show that thou art kind.

Awake in us compassion,
O Lord of life divine;
create in us thy spirit;
give us a love like thine.
Help us to seek thy kingdom
that cometh from above,
and in thy great salvation,
show forth thy boundless love.

Words: John W. Shackford (1878-1969)
Source: "Seven New Social Welfare Hymns," 1961
Possible tune: LLANGLOFFAN
Scriptural references: Matthew 18:12-14, Luke 15:3-6
Topics: Compassion, Discipleship, Faithfulness

Praise Be to Christ, the Lord of Life!

CMD

Praise be to Christ, the Lord of life!
  Through him all worlds were formed;
he is the Word that called them forth
  when light of day first dawned.
All things that are and are to be
  in him their center find;
he holds in his sustaining hands
  the life of humankind.

Praise be to Christ, the Lord of life!
  One with our human race,
he lived our life, he died our death,
  the Lord of love and grace.
He is the way that leads to God,
  the truth that sets us free;
he is the life, he offers life
  to all humanity.

Praise be to Christ, the Lord of life!
  In his blest company
brothers and sisters in the faith
  find their true unity.
From him the Church receives her life,
  by him her steps are led,
on him alone her hope is fixed;
  he is her sovereign head.

Praise be to Christ, the Lord of life!
  His power let us proclaim,
till all acknowledge him as Lord,
  and all exalt his name.
Pray, sisters, brothers in the faith,
  pray that his kingdom come,
when all shall find true life in him
  and all in him be one.

Words: Harmon B. Ramsey (b. 1907)
Source: *The Hymn* 34:156 (July 1983)
Possible tunes: KINGSFOLD, REGWAL
Scriptural references: John 1:1-2, John 14:6
Topics: Church, Jesus Christ, Unity

Praise to the Lord Who on This Day of Days

10 10 10 with alleluias

Praise to the Lord who on this day of days
has brought to us salvation, love, and grace;
no words can tell our joy, no tune or phrase.
Alleluia, alleluia!

Let sun and star shine forth in splendor bright;
let sky and earth proclaim spring-time delight,
as tree and flower bring blossom into sight.
Alleluia, alleluia!

New life and love are joined in mutual tone
to hail the King whose victory has won
our full salvation: that's what Christ has done.
Alleluia, alleluia!

Arise, O saints and join the mighty throng
to tell the world what Christ our Lord has done,
lift up your voice and join the joyful song.
Alleluia, alleluia!

Words: W. Melvin Maxey (b. 1927)
Source: *The Hymn* 24:1 (January 1973)
Possible tunes: SINE NOMINE, FREDERICKTOWN
Topics: Easter/Resurrection

Proclaim New Hope Through Christ Our Lord

87 87 887

Proclaim new hope through Christ our Lord;
    the Savior now provides it.
For future days, in plenteous ways
    our hope in him sustains us.
Christ calls us to unwavering love,
commitment to those highest goals,
    and to the cause most noble.

Proclaim new power—a challenge strong
    to draw upon the Spirit.
Great strength is ours to do his will
    when we our weakness measure.
For who can know and who can see
what miracles may come to be
    when in his power we labor?

Proclaim to all the Church of Christ—
    the world awaits our witness!
O that we may in every way
    touch lives of those around us.
Responding to God's call this hour,
enabled by the Spirit's power,
    may we be Christ unto them.

Words: Constance Cherry, 1982 (b. 1953)
Source: *The Hymn* 33:253 (October 1982)
Possible tune: MIT FREUDEN ZART
Topics: Commitment, Hope, Witnessing

Rejoice! God Is with Us

11 11 11 11

Rejoice! God is with us, let praises resound;
the way of salvation through flesh has been found.
The advent of Jesus has banished the night;
God broke through the darkness and turned it to light!

Come hear this, all you who are lonely and blue;
what prophets have promised is proven and true.
His coming has happened; no more must we wait.
Break forth into joy and with songs celebrate!

He tenderly reaches to those who are lost,
brings blessings and pardon and counts not the cost.
The bonds of oppression are shattered and torn,
the fractures are mended, the faithless reborn.

Rejoice! God is with us, make known to the earth
the love and the splendor of Bethlehem's birth.
O marvelous coming, miraculous thing,
by way of a manger—our Savior and King!

Words: Daniel B. Merrick, Jr., 1978 (b. 1926)
Source: *The Hymn* 31:281 (October 1980)
Possible tune: ST. DENIO
Scriptural references: Matthew 1:23, Matthew 28:20b
Topics: Epiphany, Incarnation, Light

Responding to Your Call, O Lord

CMD

Responding to your call, O Lord,
  we've come here, led by grace,
where study is our offered gift,
  each desk, an altar-place.
Here need and deep commitment met
  and faithfully designed
this place for questing of the soul
  and challenge for the mind.

As servants, we would search your Word
  and search ourselves anew,
with heart and mind kept consecrate
  to humbly learn of you.
From thoughtful, patient discipline,
  create each needed skill
for scholars' minds and pastors' hearts
  apprenticed to your will.

Keep stewards of your mysteries
  from losing awe, for time
can dim the fragile edge that guards
  the sacred and sublime.
Let those who handle holy things
  be nourished by them, too,
and minister to all who serve
  in ministry with you.

Lord, as we study, live, and teach
  the truths which make us whole,
we seek to dedicate our best
  of body, mind, and soul;
then, from the years invested here
  help us proclaim your worth,
as we go forth and freely share
  Good News throughout the earth.

Words: David A. Robb (b. 1932)
Source: *The Hymn* 42:4 (October 1991)
Possible tune: KINGSFOLD
Topics: Commitment, Ministry, Prayer, Service/Servanthood, Stewardship

Sing, Children, Sing

47 57 with refrain

Sing, children, sing,
for God has made the singing;
stars sang together
when the world was very young.
Refrain:
Sing praise, alleluia
to the Father, to the Son;
sing we praise, alleluia.
In the Spirit we are one.

Dance, children, dance,
for God has made the dancing;
life, movement, rhythm
had their birth when time began.
Refrain

Laugh, children, laugh,
for God has made the laughter;
God is contentment,
God is joy, and God is love.
Refrain

God's looking down,
rejoicing with his people.
Sing to his glory!
Let your heart rejoice in him.
Refrain

Words: Audrey Schultz (b. 1940)
Source: *The Hymn* 30:216 (July 1979)
Possible tune: SING PRAISE (see p. 162)
Scriptural reference: Job 38:7, Psalm 149:1-5
Topics: Adoration and Praise, Children

Sing of a God in Majestic Divinity

12 10 12 10

Sing of a God in majestic divinity,
seeding the heavens with numberless stars,
forming our dust and our dreams of infinity,
God of our genes and the judge of our wars.

Sing of a child who was cradled so tenderly,
sing of a boyhood by Galilee's lake;
sing of a cross and a Savior who wondrously
suffered and died for humanity's sake.

Sing of a Spirit who daily addresses us,
lives in our sciences, nature, and arts;
moving through all of creation and blessing us,
guiding our minds and engaging our hearts.

Sing of this God who in glory and mystery
chooses to lie in humanity's womb,
enters the prison and pain of our history,
rises triumphant and opens the tomb.

Words: Herbert O'Driscoll, 1980 (b. 1928)
Source: *The Hymn* 32:241 (October 1981)
Possible tune: UTTINGEN (HB 33)
Topics: Creation, Presence of God, Trinity

Speak Now, O God, to Hearts Unmoved and Cold

10 10 10 10

Speak now, O God, to hearts unmoved and cold;
warn us as prophets did in days of old.
Anoint us messengers with tongues of flame,
called forth to love and serve in Jesus' name.

O grant us wisdom, Lord, your will to see;
show us the path of true humility.
May we do justly, led by mercy's hand,
obedient to your Spirit's high command.

Guide now our feet to ministries of love;
grant us compassion like to yours above.
Cause us to set the blind and captive free
to find in Christ the Lord their liberty.

Nerve us, O Lord, to face the times of strain;
our hands in loyal works of love sustain.
Help us to live, with Christ-like vision clear,
in partnership, to bring your kingdom near.

Words: M. Elmore Turner, alt. (b. 1906)
Source: "Seven New Social Welfare Hymns," 1961
Possible tune: TOULON
Topics: Ministry, Social Concerns/Welfare

Tell It! Tell It Out with Gladness

87 87 D

Tell it! Tell it out with gladness—
God's good news to every land,
sin forgiven, lives transfigured,
all in God's great loving plan.
In the Book is found the witness
to his mighty acts of yore:
listen, heed, obey, and serve him,
kneel before him and adore.

Lord, we thank thee for the treasure
hid within the sacred page.
We would be thy faithful heralds
to our deeply troubled age;
we would publish thy salvation,
ever on thy side to stand,
living, serving, giving, sending
life to quicken every land.

"Go and teach," thus spoke the Master,
risen victor from the grave.
Still he gives this great commission
to his faithful ones, and brave.
Go and tell the gospel story
of what all through Christ can be.
Send it! Send it to the nations
that God's love may set us free.

Words: Georgia Harkness, alt. (1891-1974)
Source: "Fifteen New Bible Hymns," 1966
Possible tune: HYMN TO JOY
Scriptural reference: Matthew 28:19-20
Topics: Commitment, Mission, Word of God

Thanks Be to You, O God*

88 88 88

Thanks be to you, O God above,
with whom we live in trust and love,
for guidance through the stormy years
of growth and discord, wars and fears.
  Our joyful voices now we raise
  in grateful songs of thankful praise.

Teach us to trust your providence
as future centuries commence;
with humble, contrite heart and mind
your ways to know, your will to find.
  Forgive what we have failed to do;
  help us apply our faith anew.

In this atomic age of space
as nations strive for power and place,
grant wisdom to our leaders, Lord;
may they be guided by thy word.
  Your righteous will is our desire;
  help us to feed that holy fire.

Grant that the persons we shall choose
to govern us, shall not abuse
the privilege of power we give,
but honorably before us live.
  So may we serve that all may view
  in us the image, Lord, of you.

*Original first line: Thanks be to thee, O God

Words: Hugh C. Stuntz, alt.
Source: "New Hymns for America 1976," 1975
Possible tune: DOMINUS REGNAVIT (see page 131), MELITA
Topics: Nation, Thanksgiving, Trust

The City Is Alive, O God

CMD

The city is alive, O God,
with sound of hustling feet,
with rapid change and flashing lights
the pulse through every street;
but oft there's inhumanity
behind the bright facade,
and throngs with empty, hungering hearts
cry out for help, O God.

Is it your will, O loving God,
that races live in strife?
that loneliness and greed and hate
should mark a city's life?
Do you desire one person's wealth
to keep another poor?
Must crime and slums and lust abound?
O Lord, is there no cure?

In Galilee the people heard
your servant Christ declare
through healing touch, through word and cross,
the good news of your care.
He said your heart touched every heart
that longed for peace and right,
that those bowed down by burden borne
could find your life, your light.

O God, inspire your church today
to take Christ's servant role,
to love the world, to hear its claims,
to sense its yearning soul,
to live within the marketplace,
to serve both weak and strong,
to love itself, to share its dream,
to give the world its song.

Words: William W. Reid, Jr., alt. (b. 1923)
Source: "Nine New Hymns on the Mission of the Church," 1969
Possible tunes: ELLACOMBE, OLD IVY (see p. 146)
Topics: Church, City, Healing, Justice, Mission,
Service/Servanthood

The Earth, O Lord, Belongs to Thee

LM

The earth, O Lord, belongs to thee:
the fertile land, the sky, the sea.
O give us wisdom in our age
to hold in trust our heritage.

Let flowing rivers, deep and clear,
refresh our lives from year to year.
From streams defiled we shall reclaim
a cup of water in thy name.

May every creature in thy care,
that lives on land or soars in air,
behold the sun, the distant shore,
and breathe the breath of life once more.

In city street and country side,
may beauty, life, and health abide.
Lo, all the wastelands of our earth
await the day of second birth.

Words: Chester E. Custer (b. 1920)
Source: *The Hymn* 21:75 (July 1970)
Possible tunes: ROCKINGHAM, DUKE STREET
Scriptural references: Psalm 24:1, Romans 8:21
Topics: Earth, Ecology/Environment, Stewardship

The God of Grace

66 66 88

The God of grace be blessed!
So humbly drew he near,
by all our woes oppressed,
love put to flight our fear:
no force below, no power above,
can bar our hearts against God's love.

Our mighty God be praised,
and be his Name adored!
From death's dark hold he raised
our ever-living Lord,
who, trampling under foot the night,
brought immortality to light.

Thanksgiving render God!
He freedom gives from chains
when in our dusty clod
Christ's Holy Spirit reigns.
Henceforth no more in vain we strive;
in Christ shall all be made alive.

To God the only wise
glory and honor yield!
Beneath his healing eyes
his children he will shield
and every hurtful thing destroy,
to bring us faultless home with joy.

Words: John Underwood Stephens, 1953 (b. 1901)
Source: *The Hymn* 10:104 (October 1959)
Possible tune: OGUNQUIT (see p. 144)
Scriptural reference: I Corinthians 15:22
Topics: Adoration and Praise, Grace, Thanksgiving

The Heart Is Moved by One Supreme Desire

10 10 10 10 10 10

The heart is moved by one supreme desire:
in cold and darkness it will yet aspire
to seek the source of wondrous warmth and light,
to find the realm that is forever bright.
"O heart, draw near," so sings the heavenly choir.
"Your place is here, beside the altar fire."

The heart responds, and as it opens wide
the light and warmth come in and there abide.
The light is Christ; his outstretched hands will bring
new life to all; with joy they now can sing:
"My heart is strangely warmed, my faith will soar;
I trust in thee alone, forevermore!"

Words: Lucia Myers, 1973 (1903-1987)
Source: *The Hymn* 24:57 (April 1973)
Possible tunes: SONG 1, YORKSHIRE
Topics: Faithfulness, Light

The Lord of All Creation

14 14 14 14

The Lord of all creation moved o'er earth's primeval fire,
and from a flaming planet formed a continent entire.
He moulded its magnificence with artistry sublime,
and gilded it with glory through the majesty of time.

The love of God all passionate enfolds the pregnant earth,
and in that yearly ecstasy gives seed and season birth.
That flaming love has pierced into the world's awaiting womb,
and scattered rich resources in the subterranean gloom.

The Lord of time brought forth a race to roam the endless plain
and led a pilgrim people to forsake an old world's pain.
The God of liberation led the slave to freedom's hill,
that all may walk a way of peace and do his sovereign will.

O God, who in this land has forged a power before unknown,
yet who did mount on Calvary a sacrificial throne:
so mingle peace and justice that a people's soul may flower,
and hold us hostage in your love that we may know your power.

Words: Herbert O'Driscoll, alt. (b. 1928)
Source: *The Hymn* 33:51 (January 1982)
Possible tune: THANKSGIVING (see p. 169)
Topics: Creation, Justice, Love, Peace

The Peace of Heaven Is on Our Fields

LM

The peace of heaven is on our fields,
at your great table we are fed;
the feast of life is nobly set;
you give to us our daily bread.

And when the day dims late and chill,
and twilight fills with homing wings,
for home and love we thank you, Lord,
and all our dear familiar things.

Lord Jesus, come and be our guest,
now tarry with us in your grace
that we with burning hearts may hear
your gentle voice and see your face.

Words: J. Edgar Park, alt. (1880-1956)
Source: "Fourteen New Rural Hymns," 1955
Possible tune: OLDEN LANE (see p. 149)
Scriptural reference: Luke 24:28-32
Topics: Grace, Home and Family, Rural Life

The Son of God, Our Christ

10 10 10 10

The Son of God, our Christ, the Word, the Way,
shared human life and toiled throughout the day;
from common folk he called the twelve to be
co-workers in his sacred ministry.

In every test, in trials manifold,
these servants witnessed, by their faith made bold;
and with the gifts and talents which they brought,
the Church was founded and God's message taught.

Today, as then, Christ summons us to dare
his path to follow and his work to share,
to help and heal the sick, the lame, the blind,
to make his Gospel known to humankind.

In city street, in town, or on the soil,
may each serve Christ in faithful daily toil,
and in each thought and kindly word and deed
obey Christ's call, and go where he shall lead.

Where'er we find, our witness should be made,
whate'er our task, be thou, O Christ, our aid,
that we may gladly give for thee our best
and find each task divinely sent and blest.

Words: Edward M. Blumenfeld, alt., 1956 (b. 1927)
Source: "Three More New Hymns for Youth by Youth," 1957
Possible tune: TOULON
Topics: Commitment, Service/Servanthood, Witnessing, Youth

They Asked, "Who's My Neighbor"

11 8 11 88

They asked, "Who's my neighbor and whom should I love;
for whom should I do a good deed?"
The Master related a story and said,
"It's anyone who has a need,
yes, anyone who has a need."

There once was a traveler set on by thieves
who beat him and left him to die;
a Priest and a Levite each saw him in pain,
but they turned away and walked by,
yes, they turned away and walked by.

A certain Samaritan then came along
to bind up his wounds and give aid;
he took him to stay at an inn until well,
and for all the service he paid,
yes, for all the service he paid.

I know who's my neighbor and whom I should love,
for whom I should do a good deed;
for Christ made it clear in the story he told:
it's anyone who has a need,
yes, anyone who has a need.

Words: Jan Wesson, 1981
Source: "New Hymns for Children," 1982
Possible tune: WHO'S MY NEIGHBOR (see p. 172)
Scriptural reference: Luke 10:29-37
Topics: Children, Ministry, Service/Servanthood, Word of God

Through All the World

10 4 66 66 10 4

Through all the world let every nation sing
to God the King.
As Lord may Christ preside
where now he is defied,
and sovereign place his throne
in lands not yet his own.
Through all the world let every nation sing
to God the King.

Through all the world let everyone express
true righteousness.
May Christ now be the norm
to which we all conform,
his passion cure the sin
that festers from within.
Through all the world let everyone express
true righteousness.

Through all the world let everyone embrace
the gift of grace.
May Christ's great light consume
our darkest cities' gloom;
may Christ's great love efface
hostilities of race.
Through all the world let everyone embrace
the gift of grace.

If all the world in every part shall hear,
and God revere,
we must be moved to care
and in his name to share
the liberating word
which must be told abroad.
Then all the world in every part shall hear,
and God revere.

Words: Bryan Jeffery Leech, alt. (b. 1931)
Source: *The Hymn* 21:68 (July 1970)
Possible tune: CONRAD (see p. 126)
Topics: Grace, International Life, Sovereignty, Witnessing

Walk Softly in Springtime

11 11 11 11

Walk softly in springtime, to hear the grass sing
its whispering carols to Jesus our King,
to see the new flowers, bright colors display
to tell all the children of glad Easter Day.

Sing gently in springtime, and join with the birds,
who warble their music, a song without words,
that floats through the air and that reaches the sky,
a message of love to the Father on high.

Praise gladly in springtime when earth seems to glow
with new life and color in all things that grow;
for all nature's children are happy to say:
Rejoice, for the Savior is risen today!

Words: Edna Fay Grant (1905-1981)
Source: "Twelve New Hymns for Children," 1965
Possible tune: MARCHE DOUCEMENT (HB 470)
Topics: Children, Creation, Easter/Resurrection

We Bring the Little Children

76 76 D

We bring the little children
  to this, your church, O Lord,
baptizing them with water,
  your Spirit and your Word.
As Jesus showed his caring
  for those in years so young,
help us in all our sharing,
  show them the faith begun.

Remind us, Lord, when seeing
  all children here baptized,
of vows made for our living,
  of hope and faith realized.
Refresh us in commitment
  to Christ's redeeming ways,
and bring us to fulfillment
  as we live out our days.

Words: Gilbert Taverner (b. 1920)
Source: *The Hymn* 27:1 (January 1976)
Possible tune: ELLACOMBE
Topics: Baptism/Consecration, Children, Christian
  Nurture/Education

We Gather at Thy Table, Lord

CM

We gather at thy table, Lord,
    to fellowship with thee,
in keeping with thy will and word,
    that we may faithful be.

Now let us take the sacred bread,
    our souls and bodies feed;
in heart and soul we shall be fed,
    thy holy will to heed.

Now let us take the wine of heaven,
    for thee whose blood was shed;
that here we meet with sins forgiven,
    and by thy grace are led.

To thee, O Lord, we sing our song,
    renewed by strength divine,
for we by faith to thee belong,
    forever to be thine.

Words: Wade Alexander Mansur (b. 1890)
Source: *The Hymn* 22:12 (January 1971)
Possible tunes: DUNDEE, ST. PETER
Topics: Communion, Witnessing

We Gather at Your Table, Lord

CMD

We gather at your table, Lord,
 because you bid us come.
Our lives, though scattered through the week,
 we now unite as one.
Before us is the bread, the wine;
 prepare our souls to eat.
Come join us by your Spirit, Lord,
 and make the feast complete.

Remind us of our sacred past,
 our roots in Israel's soil.
Refresh us with your presence now
 as through today we toil.
And point us toward the future, Lord,
 your kingdom we would know,
and for our friends around us here,
 our hearts in love would grow.

We gather as your people, Lord;
 you call, and we must heed.
Our power by itself is weak;
 it is your strength we need.
Your Spirit dwell within our hearts;
 your voice speak loud and clear,
and fill us with your power and might
 as we assemble here.

Into the world again we take
 your covenant of grace.
Refreshed by taking time to pause
 from our own selfish pace.
May love be ours and overflow
 that all the world may see
that you will be our holy God,
 your people we will be.

Words: William Martin, 1971, rev. 1979
Source: *The Hymn* 31:62 (January 1980)
Possible tunes: KINGSFOLD, FOREST GREEN
Topics: Communion, Faith

We Praise You, God, for Truth Received

CMD

We praise you, God, for truth received
from generations past,
for knowledge, gift beyond compare,
the ages have amassed.
We offer thanks for patient toil
of thinkers who assailed
the ignorance that darkens truth
and keeps its presence veiled.

But you have formed the human mind
to follow truth beyond
old boundaries and beckon us
toward knowledge yet unfound.
Let neither fear nor weariness
subvert the ardent quest
that sets our feet on paths untrod
and robs our hearts of rest.

O Wisdom, source of human thought,
in whom our questing ends;
O Truth, whose endless mystery
all human truth transcends:
teach us that, when we offer you
the best our minds have wrought,
we bring but truth your mind has known,
but wisdom you have taught.

O Christ, in whom the truth took flesh
and dwelt in time and space,
in whom God's wisdom walked our ways
and wore a human face:
the life you lived, the death you died
teach knowledge far above
our own and call our hearts to see
the crown of truth is love.

Words: Herman G. Stuempfle, Jr. (b. 1923)
Source: *The Hymn* 42:4 (October 1991)
Possible tune: KINGSFOLD
Scriptural reference: John 1:14
Topics: Truth, Wisdom

We Want to Know, Lord, Touch Our Minds

LM

We want to know: Lord, touch our minds;
we want to see, so touch our eyes.
Dispel the dark which now confines,
and help us hear the haunting cries.

We want to feel: Lord, touch our hearts,
and touch our hands that we may serve
to strengthen life in all its parts;
give courage, love, and steady nerve.

We want to act: Lord, come, inspire
these lives of ours; Lord, cleanse, refine,
empower our lives with holy fire
that we may know your will divine.

Words: Carlton C. Buck, alt. (b. 1907)
Source: "Ten New Hymns for the 70's," 1970
Possible tune: LLEF (PsH 137), WAREHAM
Topics: Courage, Service/Servanthood

Where Restless Crowds Are Thronging

76 76 D

Where restless crowds are thronging
along the city ways,
where pride and greed and turmoil
consume the fevered days,
where vain ambitions banish
all thoughts of praise and prayer,
the people's spirits waver:
but you, O Christ, are there.

In scenes of want and sorrow
and haunts of flagrant wrong,
in homes where kindness falters,
and strife and fear are strong,
in busy streets of barter,
in lonely thoroughfare,
the people's spirits languish:
but you, O Christ, are there.

With bombing and fierce burning
your people find no peace.
Help us to share their yearning
that senseless death may cease.
Break through our ease and comfort,
forbid that we not care;
and strengthen all our efforts:
for you, O Christ, are there.

O Christ, behold your people—
they press on every hand!
bring light to all the cities
of our divided land.
May all our bitter striving
give way to visions fair
of righteousness and justice:
for you, O Christ, are there.

Words: Thomas Curtis Clark, alt. (1877-1953)
Source: "Five New Hymns on the City," 1954
Possible tune: LLANGLOFFAN
Topics: City, Incarnation, Jesus Christ, Justice

Within the Shelter of Our Walls

86 886

Within the shelter of our walls,
    be present, Lord, to guide.
Where work is planned, where pleasure calls,
where hearts keep holy festivals,
    find welcome, and abide.

Transform our spirits as we learn,
    your loving discipline.
When tasks are hard or duty stern,
give us the wisdom to discern
    true fellowship within.

Make daily bread a sacrament
    which you, O Lord, will share.
Give conversation high intent;
our daily strength for you be spent
    with thought and loving care.

Words: Elinor Lennen, alt. (b. 1900)
Source: "Thirteen New Marriage and Family Life Hymns," 1961
Possible tunes: REST, REPTON
Topics: Guidance, Home and Family,
    Weddings/Christian Marriage, Wisdom

Word of God, Across the Ages

87 87 D

Word of God, across the ages
    comes your message to our life:
source of hope forever present
    in our toil and fears and strife;
constant witness to God's mercy,
    still our grace whate'er befall;
guide unfailing, strength eternal,
    offered freely to us all;

story of the wondrous journey
    from the shadows of the night;
garnered truth of sage and prophet,
    guiding forward into light;
words and deeds of Christ our Master,
    pointing to the life and way,
still appealing, still inspiring,
    'mid the struggles of today.

In the tongues of all the peoples
    may the message bless and heal
as devout and patient scholars
    more and more its depths reveal.
Bless, O God, both wise and simple
    with your truth of ageless worth,
till all lands receive the witness
    and your knowledge fills the earth.

Words: Ferdinand Q. Blanchard, 1952, alt. (1876-1968)
Source: "Ten New Hymns on the Bible," 1952
Possible tunes: ABBOT'S LEIGH, BLAENWERN
Topics: Adoration and Praise, Witnessing, Word of God

You Called Me, Father, By My Name

CM

*You called me, Father, by my name
 when I had still no say;
today you call me to confirm
 the vows my parents made.

You give me freedom to believe;
 today I make my choice,
and to the worship of the church
 I add my learning voice.

Within the circle of the faith,
 as member of your cast,
I take my place with all the saints
 of future, present, past.

In all the tensions of my life,
 between my faith and doubt,
let your great Spirit give me hope,
 sustain me, lead me out.

So help me in my unbelief
 and let my life be true:
feet firmly planted on the earth,
 my sights set high on you.

*An alternative first stanza is offered where a person has not been baptized in infancy:

Lord, when I came into this life,
 you called me by my name;
today I come, commit myself,
 responding to your claim.

The hymn can also be sung in the first person plural.

Words: Fred Kaan (b. 1926)
Source: "Three Hymns for 1979," 1979
Possible tunes: WINCHESTER OLD, DUNFERMLINE,
 CONFIRMATION (*Hymnal Supplement* 29)
Scriptural reference: Isaiah 43:1
Topics: Baptism/Consecration, Confirmation, Commitment

You Never Saw Old Galilee

CM or 86 866

You never saw old Galilee
so friendly and so fair.
My mates and I sang merrily
and never had a care,
and never had a care.

Out where the sea runs green and cold
and many fathoms deep,
I called my mates, "Look in the hold!
The Master's gone asleep!
The Master's gone asleep!"

And then the clouds grew grim and black;
there blew an awful gale.
"Heave to, my mates, the mast will crack,
if we don't lower the sail,
if we don't lower the sail!"

The rain poured down, the waves leapt high,
the winds they whipped us round
and tossed us toward the terrible sky
and roared their terrible sound,
and roared their terrible sound.

We roused the Master from his sleep
and called his name in dread:
"Come save us from the awful deep
or we're as good as dead,
or we're as good as dead!"

Then up he stood against the gale,
  and told the storm to cease.
Tempestuous winds broke off their wail;
  waves calmed and lay at peace,
  waves calmed and lay at peace.

So, friends, although the sea be wide
  and though your boat be small,
there's naught to fear from time or tide;
  the Master's Lord of all,
  the Master's Lord of all.

Then sing, my friends, sing merrily;
  O sing both bold and brave.
The One who made the surging sea
  still rules the wind and wave,
  still rules the wind and wave.

Words: Herman G. Stuempfle, Jr. (b. 1923),
  based on Mark 4:35-41
Source: *The Hymn* 40:31 (July 1989)
Possible tune: PETER'S CHANTY (see p.150)
Scriptural reference: Matthew 8:23-27, Mark 4:35-41
Topics: Discipleship, Jesus Christ, Saints, Word of God

ABBA

LM

Music: Allen Sampson, 1980
Words: Charles Coffin, 1736; tr. John Chandler, 1837
Source: *The Hymn* 37:171 (July 1981)

ANNIE LYTLE

88 88 88 88 88

Music: Lloyd Pfautsch (b. 1921)
Words: Jaroslav J. Vajda (b. 1919)
Source: "Three Hymns for 1979"

way, you sought us lost and fu - gi - tive. You changed our
cried, you made the griefs of mour- ners cease, gave Sa - tan's
than that we re - flect our Fath - er's face. Show us the
still will die and dies with- out your dew. Since God is
wills from "must" to "may," you calm us with your "I for -
prey a place to hide. Who sees you on your cross- bound
depth and height and span of love that spares no sac - ri -
love, and an - gels thrill to find this won - der ev - er
give," and all our fears are soothed a - way. It is by
knees, sees love that can - not be de - nied. This kind of
fice, and we shall do what you be - gan: reach to the
new, his gra- cious will help us ful - fill, and join his

love that we sur - vive. Lord, as you taught us once to
love in us in - crease. As you for love were cru - ci -
world with your em - brace. As you o- beyed your Fa - ther's
joy - ful re - ti - nue. Lord, as in love you saw God's
pray, so teach us now in love to live.
fied, so teach us, Lord, that way to peace.
plan, make us such ves - sels of your grace.
will, so make that love, that will, ours too.

BENJAMIN

10 10 10 10

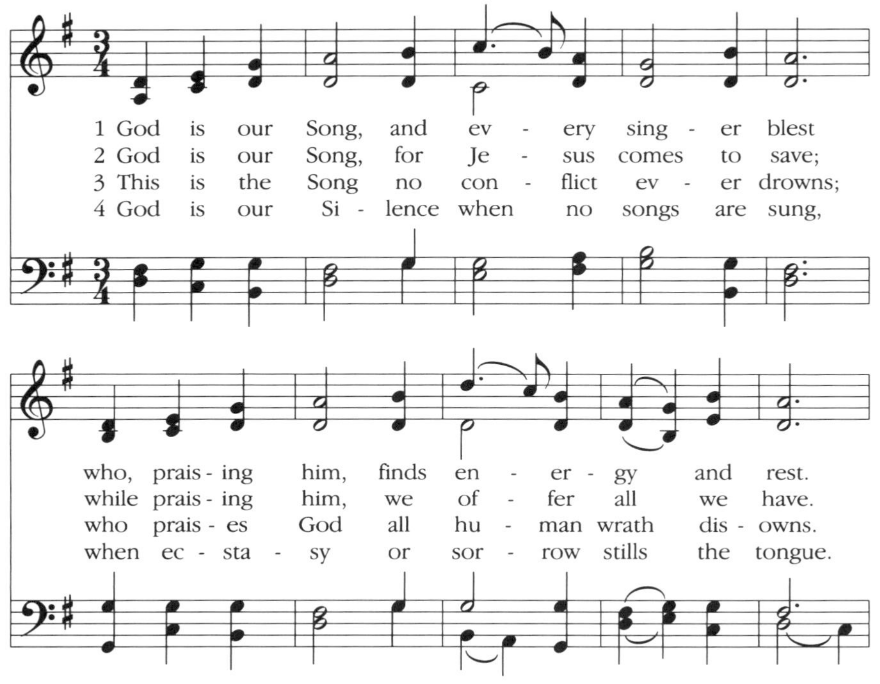

Music: Alfred V. Fedak, 1986 (b. 1953)
Words: Fred Pratt Green, 1976 (b. 1903)
Source: *The Hymn* 38:34 (January 1987)

All who praise God with un - af - fect - ed joy
New songs we sing, in ven - tures new u - nite,
Love knows what rich com - plex - i - ties of sound
Glo - rious the faith which si - lent - ly o - beys
give back to us the wis - dom we de - stroy.
when Je - sus leads us up - ward in - to light.
God builds up - on a sim - ple, com - mon ground.
un - til we find a - gain the voice of praise.

COKE-JEPHCOTT

10 10 10 10

Music: James Boeringer, 1958 (b. 1930)
Words: James Boeringer, 1957, alt.
Source: *The Hymn* 10:64 (April 1959)

grant the pe - ti - tion of each heart sin - cere:
to steal our peace and joy, help each to pray:
our souls make hum - ble till we cry to thee:
de - stroy temp - ta - tion's power and hear each plea:
till faith shall lead to sight, our prayer shall be:
"Lord, I be - lieve; help thou mine un - be - lief."
"Lord, I be - lieve; help thou mine un - be - lief."
"Lord, I be - lieve; help thou mine un - be - lief."
"Lord, I be - lieve; help thou mine un - be - lief."
"Lord, I be - lieve; help thou mine un - be - lief."

CONRAD

10 4 66 66 10 4

Music: Paul Liljestrand (b. 1931)
Words: Bryan Jeffery Leech, alt. (b. 1931)
Source: *The Hymn* 21:68 (July 1970)

now he is de - fied and sov - ereign place his
which we all con - form, his pas - sion cure the
dark - est cit - ies' gloom; may Christ's great love ef -
in his name to share the lib - er - a - ting
throne in lands not yet his own. Through all the
sin that fes - ters from with - in. Through all the
face hos - til - i - ties of race. Through all the
word which must be told a - broad. Then all the
world let ev - ery na - tion sing to God the King.
world let ev - ery - one ex - press true right - eous - ness.
world let ev - ery - one em - brace the gift of grace.
world in ev - ery part shall hear, and God re - vere.

DENTON

888 888 with alleluias

Music: Joe Pinson, 1980 (b. 1937)
Words: St. Francis of Assisi, 1225; tr. William H. Draper, c. 1910
Source: *The Hymn* 32:108 (April 1981)

with soft - er gleam! O praise him, O praise him.
Al - le - lu - ia! Al - le - lu - ia!

DOMINUS REGNAVIT

88 88 88

Music: Gerre Hancock, 1974 (b. 1934)
Words: Hugh C. Stuntz, alt.
Music source: *The Hymn* 31:131 (April 1980)
Words Source: "New Hymns for America: 1976," 1975

for gui- dance through the storm - y years of growth and
with hum- ble, con - trite heart and mind your ways to
grant wis- dom to our lea - ders, Lord; may they be
the priv - i - lege of power we give, but hon - or -
dis - cord, wars and fears. Our joy - ful
know, your will to find. For - give what
guid - ed by your word. Your right - eous
ably be - fore us live. So may we

voi - ces now we raise in grate - ful songs of
we have failed to do; help us ap - ply our
will is our de - sire; help us to feed that
serve that all may view in us the i - mage,
1, 2, 3
4
thank - ful praise.
faith a - new.
ho - ly fire.
Lord, of you.

FAXON

LM

Music: David W. Music, 1980 (b. 1949)
Words: S. B. Monsell, 1863
Source: *The Hymn* 32:170 (July 1981)

Christ thy right; lay hold on life and
Last time to Coda
it shall be thy joy and crown e - ter - nal - ly.
Coda
ly.

FORLINES

CM

Music: Wilbur Held (b. 1914)
Words: Carlton C. Buck, alt.
Music Source: *The Hymn* 26:91 (July 1975)
Words Source: "Nine New Hymns on the Mission of the Church," 1969

HAWLEY

CM

Music: Alice Parker (b. 1925)
Words: Fred Kaan (b. 1926)
Source: "Three Hymns for 1979," 1979

LIFE OF THE WORLD

569 669

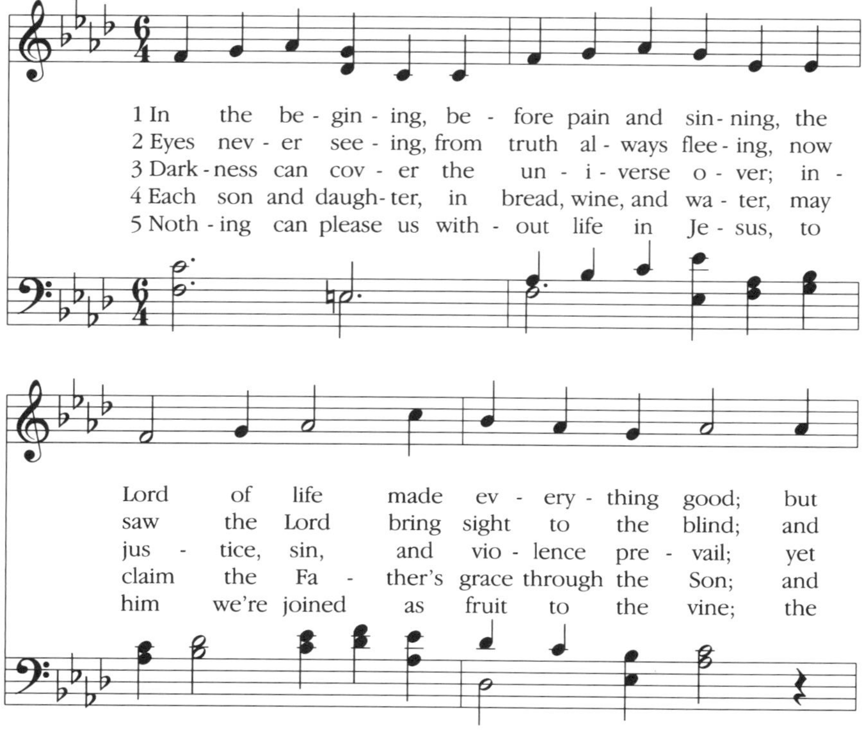

Music: Austin C. Lovelace, 1983 (b. 1919)
Words: Rae E. Whitney, 1983 (b. 1927)
Source: *The Hymn* 34:158 (July 1983)

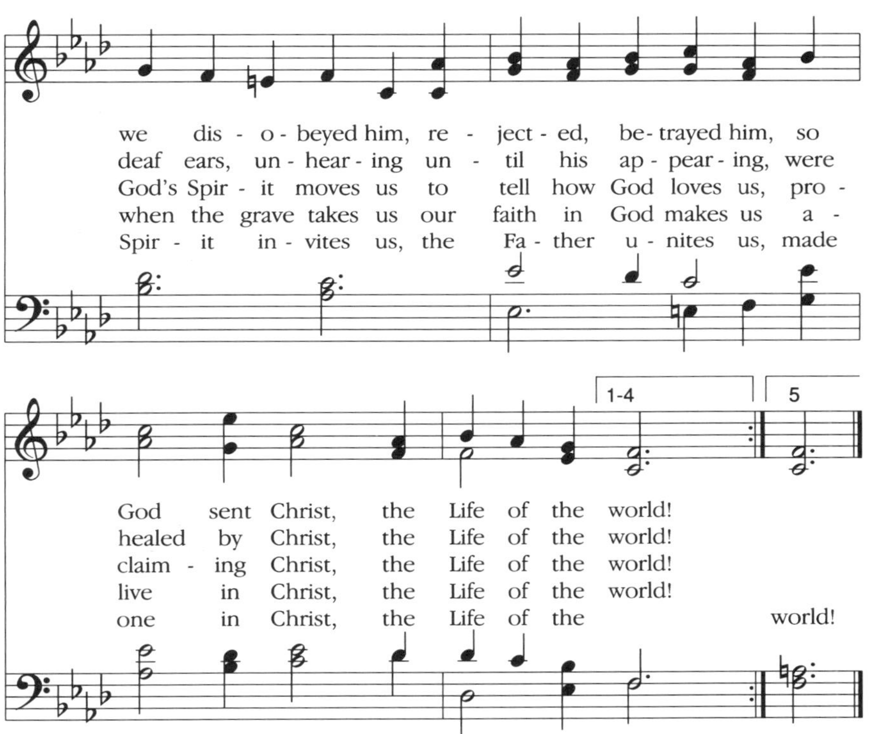
we dis - o - beyed him, re - ject - ed, be - trayed him, so
deaf ears, un - hear - ing un - til his ap - pear - ing, were
God's Spir - it moves us to tell how God loves us, pro -
when the grave takes us our faith in God makes us a -
Spir - it in - vites us, the Fa - ther u - nites us, made
1-4
5
God sent Christ, the Life of the world!
healed by Christ, the Life of the world!
claim - ing Christ, the Life of the world!
live in Christ, the Life of the world!
one in Christ, the Life of the world!

MOUNTAIN BROOK

87 87 D

Music: Wilbur Held (b. 1914)
Words: William W. Reid, Jr. (b. 1923)
Source: *The Hymn* 27:124 (October 1976)

all a - round us! Ju - bi - la - te! Sing for joy!
word pro- claimed it. Ju - bi - la - te! Sing for joy!
world a - round us! Ju - bi - la - te! Sing for joy!
work to - geth - er. Ju - bi - la - te! Sing for joy!
Man.
Help us, God, pre - serve earth's splen - dor for to -
Save us, God, from waste - ful liv - ing, from pol -
May no greed or war - ring mad - ness scorch the
Part - ners work - ing till as stew - ards we can
Ped.
mor - row's world to see.
lu - tion's tra - ge - dy.
earth or rob our bread.
say "Earth's good!" once more. A - men.

NEW YORK AVENUE

77 77 77

Music: Stephen H. Prussing, 1980
Words: Scott S. Pierpoint, 1864
Source: *The Hymn* 32:110 (April 1981)

OGUNQUIT

66 66 88

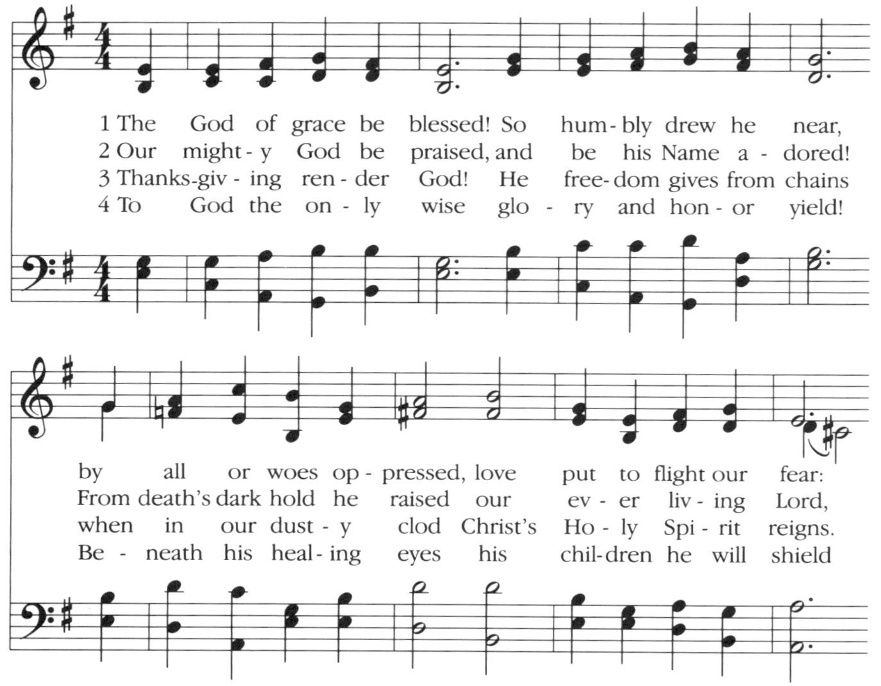

Music: Seth Bingham, 1952 (1882-1972)
Words: John Underwood Stephens, 1953 (b. 1901)
Source: *The Hymn* 10:104 (October 1959)

no force be - low, no power a - bove, can
who, tramp - ling un - der foot the night, brought
Hence - forth no more in vain we strive; in
And ev - ery hurt - ful thing de - stroy, to
bar our hearts a - gainst God's love.
im - mor - tal - i - ty to light.
Christ shall all be made a - live.
bring us fault - less home with joy. A - men.

OLD IVY

CMD

Music: Lee H. Bristol, Jr. (1923-1979)
Words: William W. Reid, Jr., alt. (b.1923)
Music source: *The Hymn* 6:131 (October 1955)
Words source: "Nine New Hymns on the Mission of the Church." 1969

oft there's in - hu - man - i - ty be - hind the
you de - sire one per - son's wealth to keep a -
said your heart touched ev - ery heart that longed for
live with - in the mar - ket - place, to serve both
bright fa - cade, and throngs with emp - ty,
noth - er poor? Must crime and slums and
peace and right, that those bowed down by
weak and strong, to love it - self, to
hun - gering hearts cry out for help, O God.
lust a - bound? O Lord, is there no cure?
bur - den borne could find your life, your light.
share its dream, to give the world its song.

OLDEN LANE

LM

Music: Lee H. Bristol, Jr., 1956 (1923-1979)
Words: J. Edgar Park, alt. (1880-1956)
Music source: *The Hymn* 7:100 (July 1956)
Words source: "Fourteen New Rural Hymns," 1955

PETER'S CHANTY

86 866

Music: Ben S. DeVan
Words: Herman G. Stuempfle, Jr. (b. 1923), based on Mark 4:45-31
Words source: *The Hymn* 40:31 (July 1989)

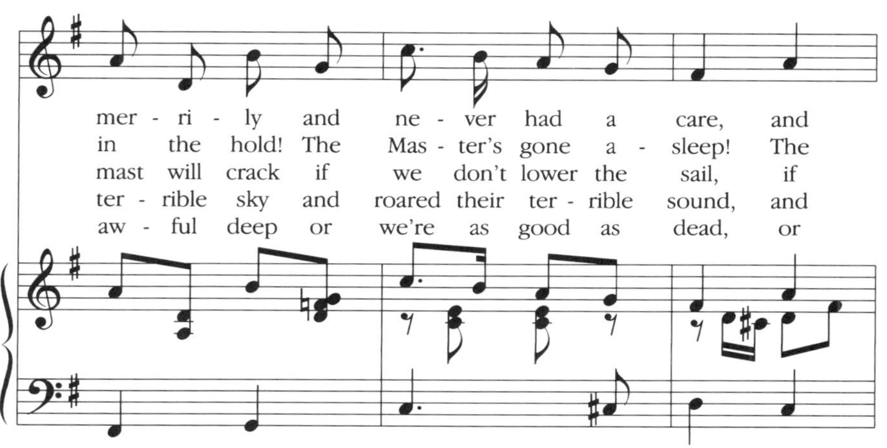

6 Then up he stood against the gale,
and told the storm to cease.
Tempestuous winds broke off their wail;
waves calmed and lay at peace,
waves calmed and lay at peace.

7 So, friends, although the sea be wide
and though your boat be small,
there's naught to fear from time or tide;
the Master's Lord of all,
the Master's Lord of all.

8 Then sing, my friends, sing merrily;
O sing both bold and brave.
The one who made the surging sea
still rules the wind and wave,
still rules the wind and wave.

PRAISE THE LORD!

CM

Music: Garry A. Cornell, 1966
Words: Psalm 148, vers. *London Foundling Hospital Collection*, 1796
Music source: *The Hymn* 18:80 (July 1967)

ROCK HARBOR

10 10 10 10

Music: Alan MacMillan (b. 1947)
Words: Hal H. Helms (b. 1923)
Music and words source: *The Hymn* 38:32 (January 1987)

Fa - ther, Son, and Spi - rit, be
all cre - a - tion join the hymn of praise: "Great
lof - ty moun - tain peaks and sigh - ing trees make
Word made flesh, Christ with us here to stay, in
Fa - ther, Son, and Spi - rit, One in Three, be
glo - ry now and to e - ter - ni - ty.
is our God in all his works and ways."
known their praise to ev - ery pass - ing breeze.
lives made ho - ly as they find your way.
glo - ry now and to e - ter - ni - ty.

RUSSELL

11 11 11 11

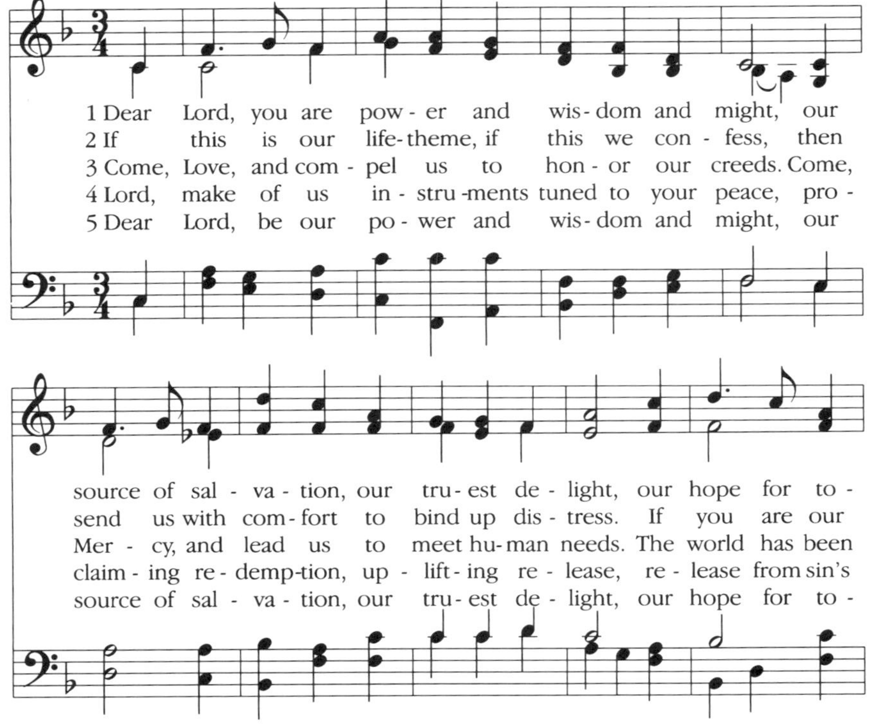

Music: David G. Mehrtens (b. 1930); harm. David L. Furniss (b. 1955)
Words: David G. Mehrtens
Music and words source: *The Hymn* 42:43 (January 1991)

mor - row, our joy for to - day, the truth and the
cit - a - del, cour - age, and song, then send us to
frac - tured, its heal - ing is late, the times are in
bur - den, from pov - er - ty's grief, with fresh air of
mor - row, our joy for to - day, the truth and the
1-3
4-5
glo - ry we share on our way.
bat - tle all e - vil and wrong.
dark - ness, the sor - row is great.
free - dom, with joy and re - lief.
glo - ry we share on our way.

ST. JUSTIN

LM

Music: Robert Hilf, 1980 (b. 1941)
Words: Isaac Watts, 1707
Music source: *The Hymn* 32:109 (April 1981)

ST. PAUL'S, ROCHESTER

11 10 11 10 10 10 10

Music and words: Jackson Hill, alt. (b. 1941)
Music and words source: *The Hymn* 29:175 (July 1978)

say - ing "O Saul, why do you per - se - cute me?
we cher - ish all the rich and bles - sed coun - sels
O grant us strength to bring a - bout the tri - umph
Re - pent, be - lieve the Fa - ther's word re - vered."
that through your Spir - it do your pres - ence prove.
of truth and mer - cy, jus - tice and the right.
Lord, send us forth from our Da - mas - cus road
Lord, send us forth in - to the world with grace,
Lord, send us forth in - to the world with joy,

that we, your church, may proud - ly name you Lord;
that we, your church, may proud - ly name you Lord;
that we, your church, may proud - ly name you Lord;
O grant us faith and cour- age e'er to be
O grant us faith and cour- age e'er to be
O grant us faith and cour- age e'er to be
fools for your sake, and guar- dians of your word.
fools for your sake, and guar- dians of your word.
fools for your sake, and guar- dians of your word.

SING PRAISE

47 57 with refrain

Music: Audrey Schultz (b. 1940); harm. Carl F. Schalk, 1979 (b. 1929)
Words: Audrey Schultz
Music and words source: *The Hymn* 30:216 (July 1979)

Sing praise, al - le - lu - ia to the Fa - ther, to the Son;
sing we praise, al - le - lu - ia. In the Spir - it we are one.
Rhythm patterns:
Triangle: all stanzas
Maracas: stanzas 2, 3, 4
Tambourine: stanzas 3, 4

SPES MUNDI

11 10 11 10

Music: Healey Willan, 1955 (1880-1968)
Words: Georgia Harkness, 1953 (1891-1974)
Music source: *The Hymn* 7:111 (October 1956)
Words source: "Twelve Ecumenical Hymns," 1954

Save us, thy peo - ple, from con - su - ming pas - sion,
still let thy Spir - it un - to us be giv - en
walk thou be - side us lest the tempt- ing by - ways
we ren - der back the love thy mer - cy gave us;
we would be faith - ful to thy gos - pel glo - rious:
who by our own false hopes and aims are spent.
to heal earth's wounds and end her bit - ter strife.
lure us a - way from thee to end - less night.
take thou our lives and use them as thou wilt.
thou art our Lord! Thou dost for - ev - er reign!

STUART

87 87

Music and words: Paul A. Richardson, 1986 (b. 1951)
Music and words source: *The Worshiping Church,* no. 778

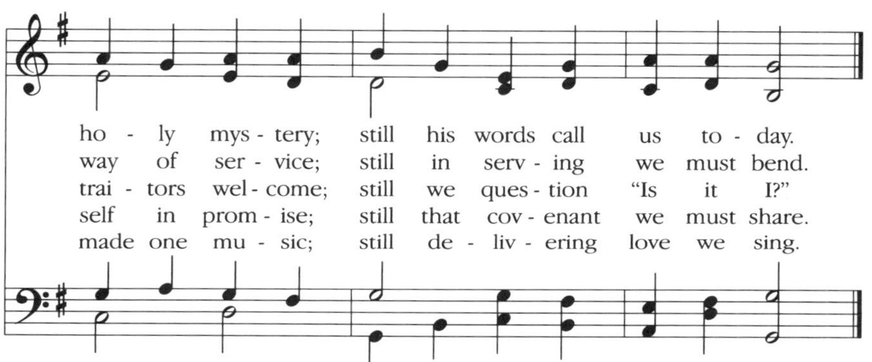

6 As he went into the garden
praying, "Father, use your Son,"
Christ alone could know its meaning;
still we pray, "God's will be done."

7 Though this feast be one of symbols,
what we celebrate is real;
still Christ welcomes to his table;
still Christ serves us at his meal.

THANKSGIVING

14 14 14 14

Music: Calvin Hampton, 1981 (1938-1984)
Words: Herbert O'Driscoll, 1981 (b. 1928)
Music and words source: *The Hymn* 33:50 (January 1982)

formed a con - tin - ent en - tire. He mold - ed
cy gives seed and sea - son birth. That flam - ing
to for - sake an old world's pain. The God of
ry a sac - ri - fi - cial throne: so min - gle
its mag - ni - fi - cence with ar - tis - try sub - lime,
love has pierced in - to the world's a - wait - ing womb,
lib - er - a - tion led the slave to free - dom's hill,
peace and jus - tice that a peo - ple's soul may flower,

and gild - ed it with glo - ry through the ma -
and scat - tered rich re - sour - ces in the sub -
that all may walk a way of peace and do
and hold us hos - tage in your love that we
1, 2, 3
4
jes - ty of time.
ter - ran - ean gloom.
his sov - ereign will.
may know your
power.
rit.
a tempo

WHO'S MY NEIGHBOR

11 8 11 88

Music and words: Jan Wesson, 1981
Music and words source: "New Hymns for Children," 1982

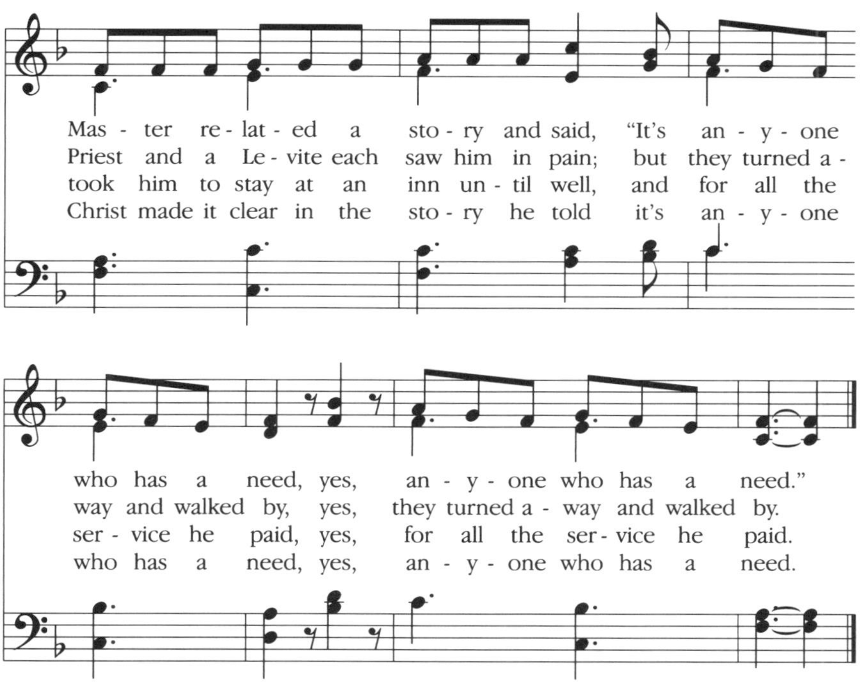
Mas - ter re - lat - ed a sto - ry and said, "It's an - y - one
Priest and a Le - vite each saw him in pain; but they turned a -
took him to stay at an inn un - til well, and for all the
Christ made it clear in the sto - ry he told it's an - y - one
who has a need, yes, an - y - one who has a need."
way and walked by, yes, they turned a - way and walked by.
ser - vice he paid, yes, for all the ser - vice he paid.
who has a need, yes, an - y - one who has a need.

WOODLANDS

88 86

Music: Seth Kasten
Words: Florence Jansson, alt.
Music source: *The Hymn* 20:124 (October 1969)
Words source: "Twelve New Hymns for Children," 1965;
The Hymn 20:124 (October 1969)

Indexes

Hymn Society Collections (1952-1982)

Holding in Trust

Hymn Society Collections (1952-1982)

1 Ten New Hymns on the Bible (1952)
2 "The Divine Gift" by Sarah E. Taylor (1952)
3 Eleven Ecumenical Hymns (1954)
4 Five New Hymns on the City (1954)
5 "Hope of the World" by Georgia Harkness (1954)
6 Fourteen New Rural Hymns (1955)
7 Five New Hymns for Youth by Youth (1955)
8 A New Hymn on the Home by Harry Emerson Fosdick ("O God, Who to a Loyal Home") (1956)
9 Two More New Hymns for Youth by Youth (1956)
10 Three More New Hymns for Youth by Youth (1957)
11 Four More New Hymns for Youth by Youth (1958)
12 Twelve New World Order Hymns (1958)
13 Fifteen New Christian Education Hymns (1959)
14 One More New Hymn for Youth by Youth (1959)
15 Seven New Social Welfare Hymns (1961)
16 Ten New Stewardship Hymns (1961)
17 Thirteen New Marriage and Family Life Hymns (1961)
18 Hymns of the Twentieth Century (1963)
19 Twelve New Hymns for Children (1965)
20 "My God Is There, Controlling" and other hymns and poems (1965)
21 Ten New Hymns on the Ministry (1966)
22 Fifteen New Bible Hymns (1966)
23 Twelve New Lord's Day Hymns (1968)
24 Nine New Hymns on the Mission of the Church (1969)
25 Ten New Hymns for the 70's (1970)
26 Seven New Hymns of Hope (1971)
27 Sixteen New Hymns on the Stewardship of the Environment (1973)
28 New Hymns, Songs and Prayers for Church and Home (1974)
29 New Hymns for America 1976 (1975)
30 Ten New Hymns on Aging and the Later Years (1976)
31 Nine Hymns for Human Relations Day (1977)
32 Three Hymns for 1979 (1979)
33 New Hymns for Children (1982)

Index of Hymn Society Collections

The number under *Source* indicates in which collection the hymn appears.
See collection titles on page 176.

First Lines

Source	First Line	Author
19	A bird, a lovely butterfly	Jansson, Florence Pedigo
19	Accept, dear God, my thanks this morn	Ryden, Ernest Edwin
12	All-knowing God, whose science charts	Reid, William Watkins
20	All weary, weary tossed the world	Reid, William Watkins
20	Almighty God, who daily art revealing	Reid, William Watkins
29	Almighty God, who made all things	Van Burkalow, Anastasia
29	America, how great the dream	Reid, William W., Jr.
29	America, my homeland fair	Lanier, H. Glen
20	And, lo, what God had made was good	Reid, William Watkins
20	Around their fires that wint'ry night	Reid, William Watkins
31	As children of one God we must	Keenze, Muriel
10	As did the Christ, we'll undertake	Ross, Dorothy Fay
16	As men of old their first fruits brought	von Christierson, Frank
17	As we before thine altar bow	Frye, Franklin P.
24	As we proclaim your Name this hour	Brooks, Paul Q.
13	As within the pillared temple	Goodman, E. Urner
20	Beaming star and angel chorus	Reid, William Watkins
17	Before thee, Lord, we join our hearts	Foltz, Mildred Harner
12	Behold his cross against the sky	Lambert, Edna A.
20	Bless, Lord, this house, its walls and room	Reid, William Watkins
28	Bless, O God, this healing place	Emurian, Ernest K.
6	Bless, O Lord, the village road	Reid, William Watkins
28	Bless, O Lord, this child of thine	Buchanan, Violet
17	Bless thou our Christian homes, O Lord	Buck, Carlton C.
21	Bless thou thy chosen sons	Drury, Miriam
26	Break, dawn divine, throughout the world!	Spivey, Raymond Byrd
1	Break forth, O living light of God	von Christierson, Frank
20	Bright the star that lights your pillow	Reid, William Watkins
20	Bright the star through stable door	Reid, William Watkins
13	Christ, by whom twelve humble men	Minga, Ann Marcus
31	Christ found a world divided	von Christierson, Frank
12	Christ of the centuries, Lord of today	Rhind, John Gray
3	Christ, to thee all hearts be lifted	von Christierson, Frank
22	Christian men, arise and give	Young, Lois Horton
28	Christmas bells with joy are ringing	Buchanan, Violet
9	Come forth, O Christian youth	Jackson, Mary Ellen
18	Come forth, O Christian youth	Jackson, Mary Ellen
17	Come, gracious Lord, to this our home	Thompson, Irene
30	Come, ye elders, those engaging	Lexow, Genevieve
19	Cradles in a manger	Hubbert, Frances Martha
27	Creator God, we give you thanks	Arner, Betty Anne J.
27	Creator God who gave the planets life	Reid, William Watkins
25	Creator God, whose glory is creation	Kenney, Alice P.
7	Creator of the universe	Hughes, J. Donald
23	Creator of the world we know	O'Brien, Mary L.
23	Day of the Lord, ordained for our repose	Edwards, Robert Lansing
29	Dear God of all creation	Hardcastle, Carrie Hitt
20	Dear Lord, to whom in other days	Reid, William Watkins
18	Declare, O heavens, the Lord of space	Edwards, Robert Lansing
19	Each year the spring puts on her gown	Hartich, Alice
20	Earth waked that morn to grief of cross	Reid, William Watkins

Composers and Hymn tunes

Authors

20	(Reid, William Watkins, cont.)	O God, ere history began
20	—	O God, to whom all nature bows
20	—	O God, whose strength is shown in thy
20	—	O holy child, O gift of love
20	—	O Holy Spirit, prophet voice
19	—	O Lord of nature, Lord of earth
20	—	O Master, in whose life both word and deed
20	—	O nation proud and bold
20	—	O Sculptor, whose immortal love
13	—	O Teacher, Master of the skill
20	—	O thou Laborer in the workshop
17	—	O thou, whose youthful years were spent
20	—	Onward from Calvary the Gospel is speeding
20	—	Our Father, from thy bounteous cruse
20	—	Our God, who down the ages longed
20	—	Our God, whose very being breathes of love
20	—	Praise we, praise we God the Lord
20	—	Sing, angel choir, make glad our night again
20	—	Spirit of God, all silent, all holy
20	—	Thank thee, God, great Master Farmer
20	—	Thanks be to God who showers on all
20	—	That morn the Holy Spirit poured
20	—	The Earth's a garden, holy, gay
20	—	The hills awake to singing
20	—	The lambs are not bleating
20	—	The Lord is my Good Shepherd
20	—	The lowly workman's humble home
20	—	The throng did press thee, Lord, to hear
13	—	Thou, Lord, whose comely strength was gained
20	—	Thou whose questing, eager boyhood
20	—	True thanks are not of words
20	—	Tune we songs to angel chorus
20	—	Wake, sons of earth, new allelujahs raise
20	—	We search the star-lit Milky Way
20	—	What wonders have found us, what glories
20	—	When suns and planets plunge through space
26	—	Where lies the Christian's hope when fear
20	—	Wide is the realm of truth
13	Reid, William W., Jr.	Help us, O Lord, to learn
28	—	Lord, at your table kneeling
28	—	Lord, who took the little children
27	—	Mountain brook with rushing waters
15	—	O God and Father of us all
12	—	O God of every nation
6	—	O God of hill and mountain
23	—	O thou God of light all-splendored
24	—	The city is alive, O God
17	—	Thy presence, Lord, brought joy and splendor
17	Reinhardt, Josephine D.	Father Eternal, we pray for thy blessing
12	Rhind, John Gray	Christ of the centuries, Lord of today
1	—	The witness of the truth
10	Ross, Dorothy Fay	As did the Christ, we'll undertake
13	Ross, Miriam Dewey	Give me the eyes to see this child
19	Ryden, Ernest Edwin	Accept, dear God, my thanks this morn
23	—	O glorious day, when thou, the God of Light
4	Schloerb, Rolland W.	Praise to thee, O God, for cities
21	Schwartz, Benjamin F.	How beautiful the footsteps
15	—	Thy call, O Christ, we hear
30	Schwerdtfeger, Lillian	Lord, who art the great Creator
13	Shackford, John Walter	O master Teacher of mankind
15	—	O thou who art the Shepherd
21	—	O thou who art eternal truth
11	Slavens, Thomas Paul	Lord, we believe; help thou our unbelief
22	Smith, Cecil Daniel	The world still waits to hear the Word
7	Smith, Nevitt Brenton	O Son of God, who at the last

Scripture References

John

Acts

Romans

I Corinthians

II Corinthians

Galatians

Ephesians

Philippians

I Thessalonians

Hebrews

James

II Peter

I John

Revelation

Topical Index

Lord's Supper (see Communion)

Love
Christmas Bells With Joy Are Ringing
For All the Love
God of All, Whose Love Surrounds Us
Let the Songs of Earth Arise
Lord, As You Taught Us Once to Pray
Lord, At Your Table Kneeling
O Lord, May Church and Home Combine
O Lord of Love
O Lord of Love and Power
The Lord of All Creation

Marriage
(see Weddings/Christian Marriage)

Ministry
For Your True Church
Hope of the World
Lord, You Have Given Your Church
O Lord, Who Came to Earth to Show
Responding to Your Call, O Lord
Speak Now, O God, to Hearts Unmoved
They Asked, "Who's My Neighbor?"

Mission
As Saints of Old Their First Fruits Brought
Hope of the World
O Lord, the Maze of Earthly Ways
O Lord, Who Came to Earth to Show
Tell It! Tell It Out with Gladness
The City is Alive, O God

Nation
God of Eagles, God of Sparrows
Lord of Nations, God Eternal
Thanks Be To You, O God

New Year/Old Year
O God, Your Constant Care and Love
Great God, We Lift Our Hearts

Offering
As Saints of Old Their First Fruits Brought
O Christ, Whose Love Has Sought
O God of Love, Who Gavest Life

Ordination (see Commitment)

Peace
Creating God, Your Fingers Trace
Dear Lord, You Are Power
From Hearts Around the World, O Lord
Good News for This New Age
Isaiah the Prophet Has Written of Old
Lead Me from Death to Life
Lord, As You Taught Us Once to Pray
O God of Every Nation
The Lord of All Creation

Pentecost (see Holy Spirit)

Power of God
Dear Lord, You Are Power
Eternal God, Whose Power Upholds

Praise (see Adoration and Praise)

Prayer
Eternal Spirit of the Living Christ
Father Eternal, We Pray For Your Blessing
For Your True Church
Glorious Is Thy Name, Most Holy
God Almighty, God Eternal
God of All, Whose Love Surrounds Us
God, the Lord of Lowly Places
Guide Us, O God, in Paths of Truth
Lord, As You Taught Us Once to Pray
Lord, at Your Table Kneeling
Lord, We Bring to You Our Children
Lord, When I Stand, No Path Before Me
Make Us, O God, A Church That Shares
O Father, Son and Holy Spirit, Hear
Responding to Your Call, O Lord

Presence of God
Loving Spirit
O Lord of Love and Power
Sing of a God in Majestic Divinity

Reconciliation
Eternal Christ, Who, Kneeling

Resurrection (see Easter)

Righteousness of God
Glorious Is Thy Name, Most Holy
Go Forth, Strong Word of God

Rural Life
God of the Fertile Fields
O God, Your Rolling Fields Declare
O Lord, You Taught Beside the Sea
The Peace of Heaven is on Our Fields

Saints
Break Forth, O Living Light of God
Come Now and Praise the Humble Saint
Lord, When I Stand, No Path Before Me
O Lord of Love
You Never Saw Old Galilee

Salvation
Good News for This New Age
Lift Up Your Eyes

Scripture (see Word of God)

Author and Composer Index

Metrical Index

(continued)

Metrical Index–Tunes

CM (86 86) FORLINES

HAWLEY

PRAISE THE LORD!

CMD (86 86 D) OLD IVY

LM (88 88) ABBA

FAXON

OLDEN LANE

ST. JUSTIN

47 57 with refrain SING PRAISE

569 669 LIFE OF THE WORLD

66 66 88 OGUNQUIT

77 77 77 NEW YORK AVENUE
86 866 PETER'S CHANTY
87 87 STUART
87 87 D MOUNTAIN BROOK
88 86 WOODLANDS
88 88 88 DOMINUS REGNAVIT
888 888 with alleluias DENTON
88 88 88 88 88 ANNIE LYTLE
10 4 66 66 10 4 CONRAD

10 10 10 10 BENJAMIN
COKE-JEPHCOTT
ROCK HARBOR
11 8 11 88 WHO'S MY NEIGHBOR
11 10 11 10 SPES MUNDI
11 10 11 10 10 10 10
ST. PAUL'S, ROCHESTER
11 11 11 11 RUSSELL
14 14 14 14 THANKSGIVING

Tune Names

First Lines and Titles